22 YEARS
IN
FRONT OF BARS

DEDICATION

I would love to dedicate this book to all my family and friends. Love you all.

Second, I'd like to dedicate this book to all the Corrections Officers working in the United States of America. Working in this position, people would never understand what we go through on a daily basis.

ACKNOWLEDGEMENTS

I would like to thank my wife, kids, all my family, friends and co-workers who supported and believed in me over the 22-year time-period of the book.

CONTENTS

CHAPTER ONE

HOW DID I GET HERE?

I sit in the Dayroom for the first time. All my academy training is over. My three day one on one training is over. And I sit at the C.O's Desk, alone, with 120 inmates glancing out their doors staring at me up and down, trying to realize what type of officer I am. My heart is racing 100-miles-an-hour, trying my best not to look nervous or uncomfortable. The first question I ask myself before any other is, "Why the Hell am I here and how did I get here?" Correctional Institutions, Prisons, Jail, the Big House, the Slammer, and the Cut.

Whatever they are called, these places house US criminals. Men and women, boys and girls. Whether innocent or not innocent, these people were found guilty of some sort by the US court system. I know some may find this hard to believe, but the prison systems are not all black males (lol). It's a great big melting pot of all races and religions. All backgrounds from all societies. Whether being homeless on the streets to prominent Doctors, Lawyers, Pastors Engineers and Politicians. (And I have seen them all). Prisons have no stereotypes to get inside these walls. But once again, how did I get here and why am I here?

Baltimore City in the mid-60s, I guess was a beautiful thing. I guess so, because I was born in 1965. The first five years of my life was a blur (lol) but once I hit six years old things came to focus. I was raised in a household of two adults, my mom and stepdad. My biological father was a ghost, but he will magically appear later in this story. Also, after becoming more focused in my young youth, I realized that I have two younger sisters, Sandra and Christina. Like me my middle sister, Sandra's father was ghost, as well; but my youngest sister Christina was my stepdad's daughter, and he raised me and Sandra like we were his own. Growing up in Baltimore City as a kid in the early 70s was okay, I guess.

My mom, Alberta, worked at Mondawmin Mall in a store called Woolworth, as a waitress. My stepdad had a city job with the Mass Transit Administration (MTA), as a MTA Police Officer. And in the early 70s in Baltimore City, that was considered a good job. Yup, we were middle class (lol). Even though we lived in somewhat a decent neighborhood, we were still in an environment where an element of folk just doesn't want to do right. We lived on the west side of Baltimore City on Ashburton Street. I went to Gwynns Falls elementary school, which was a Baltimore City Public School on the West side of Baltimore City. Me, being a very quiet kid, I'd realized I was lonely.

Making childhood friends in my neighborhood and school was kind of hard, being that I was quiet and shy. It was hard trying to figure out how I fit in. Not having a lot of friends in the neighborhood left me from developing skills of playing sports games like basketball, baseball, and football. There were some fathers in the neighborhood who took their boy to youth summer baseball leagues at Forest Park, but I was left out because I didn't have that get out and play sports drive from my Stepdad.

Gwynns Falls Elementary School. I always questioned, even as a kid, why they put this school right next to a Middle school which Lemmel Junior High School was. (Hold that thought). Thinking back to elementary school, I was that average kid getting B's and C's on his report card. Maybe an A in subjects like Art and Gym. But I do remember my first real responsibility came when I was in the fourth grade and my teacher elected me to be a Crosswalk Guard. I never forgot how proud I was to get that bright orange belt that went over my chest and around my waist.

My job was to get to the school a little early and leave a little late to help kids across the busy street of Gwynns Falls Parkway, safely. To me, it was an honor; but at the same time, challenging. Of course, the elementary kids followed the rules of waiting for my sign to cross the street. But the middle school kids from Lemmel Junior High did their own thing; and once I saw them coming I knew it was time to go. Around that same time, I learned the meaning of the word Bullying.

There was this time where some of the boys in my class found a glove that belonged to another boy in the class. Right in front of him, they wouldn't give him his glove back and cut it up with scissors. After school the next day, the little boy got his older brother of course, from the junior high school to track down the boys who cut up his glove. Being I did my crossing guard duty and was in the same class with the boys, I was the only one they spotted out. Even though I had nothing to do with the cutting of the glove, they had to pick on someone. So, walking home, with my younger sisters, I was surrounded by a group of teenage boys ready to make an example of someone.

My sisters started crying in the background," Please don't beat up my brother!" I was petrified and pleaded my case. I had nothing to do with the glove; so, through the grace of God and my sisters crying, I was let go with no punches from the bullies. I was saved. The next day I approached the boys who actually did the glove cutting. Now, I was never wanting to start a fight; but I was so mad about the previous incident, especially in front of my sisters, that I had to pick on someone my own size.

The teacher saw the argument between us and realized that I was the aggressor and I was the one in trouble. My punishment crushed me. My stepdad was called to the school for a conference with the teacher; and before I knew it, my crossing guard privileges were revoked. I was really hurt. That thing they gave me - a little joy - was taken away.

This episode made me lonelier. I started staying in the house more, in my room. I started to develop the love of reading and drawing pictures from comic books. Reading Marvel and DC comics gave me joy. Superheroes like the Avengers, Defenders, X-Men, Justice League gave me strength. I remember first tracing the comic book characters on notebook paper. I remember showing my mom and sisters my artwork, and they loved it. My mom began buying me art supplies and I went from tracing to drawing the full pictures from the comics. And I must say, I got good. And as a kid, reading comics and drawing was my passion. (I could never figure out why I wasn't an Architect).

Back in the 70s, where the man of the house made a decent income, I guess he was considered middle-class. Every Christmas I remember my sisters and I got all the toys we wanted. I remember getting skateboards, bikes, Tyco racing tracks, Evil Knievel motorcycle man, G.I. Joe with the Kung Fu Grip, and of course Big Wheels. (Boy toys of the 70s, you got to love them). The problem was, we always had Christmas dinner with our extended family, who would come over our house. Cousins, of course, and by the time they left, most of my sisters and my toys were broken or missing. (lol) I learned really quick how to hide my loot before they got there. I'd develop the "not-share" syndrome. Sad but true.

The mid to late 70s. Times and Baltimore City were changing around me. Living in the Gwynns Falls area, and Ashburton Street was in a bad neighborhood; it was just a few blocks away, seeming to be changing for the worse. I remember walking to this mom and pop store near Dukeland Avenue and North Avenue to buy me and my sisters some penny candy. A few times I was approached by little stick-up dudes trying to rob me for my cash. (lol). I'd say, "Listen, all I have is a pocketful of pennies - no real cash," and they'd walk away. In the back of my mind I would say to myself "get a job".

There was a Cab Company down the street from where we lived. I would always walk fast past this place, because there would always be cabbies or cabdrivers on the side of the building rolling dice and gambling. They never messed with me, I guess because I was from the neighborhood, but had no problem asking me for dollar. Back then, Gwynns Falls Elementary went from kindergarten to the seventh grade.

I graduated from Gwynns Falls June 1978 and was pretty nervous for a couple of weeks, because my fate and destiny was now to go to Lemmel Junior High School. Even in the late 70s Lemmel was known to be a so-called bad school, was full of misguided black teens in fights, which was a common practice by these young teens (lol). So, in 78, when I graduated elementary school, there were days where I sat at home and practiced and develop my mean face (lol). I figured if I looked mean, the kids who liked to fight would stay away from me.

The whole eight years in elementary school I only was involved in two little minor incidents. First, there was the glove incident. The second occurrence… holdup! I have to tell you the story. Some boys and I were trying to impress some little girls in the school yard. We would run up a sliding board, and when we got to the top we would jump and land in the middle of the slide and slide down the rest of the way. As a young kid, trying to impress little girls you have very little common sense. A little girl gave me a little smile because of my foolish behavior. Wanting to impress her even more, my goal was to run faster up the sliding board and jump as high as I can, well I did. My speed up the slot was good, the problem was I got too much height in the air, jumped and missed the whole slide. Terrible, right? Landing on the ground hard on my butt and arm. Yup left arm broken (lol).

Anyway, with my arm in a cast, I went to school the next day. So, the second incident occurred when some little knucklehead kid had his finger in my face, laughing Ha Ha Ha Ha He He He He, you broke your arm. Not thinking I just reacted and swung and punched the little boy in the face. Mind you, not with the good arm the one with the casts. Word spread quickly throughout the school with the little kids that I was not to be messed with. I hoped that mean mugging practice and short temper would help me survive in a junior high school that is known for teens looking for fights.

Baltimore teens and the late 70s, if you got picked on or bullied you either fight or you will get picked on daily. I didn't want that kind of trouble in my life. Plus, I had to sisters two protect, as well. Believe it or not, teens in the late 70s and Baltimore were respectful, we listened to our parents and our teachers. But once we hit the streets, the peer pressure was in full effect. On the outside looking in, Baltimore City is known for the East Side and West Side. Baltimore teens could travel throughout the city, walk through neighborhoods, with little to no problems.

If my mom and stepdad would go away for a weekend, my sisters and I would stay the night over one of my three aunts' houses. It was fun to go over my Aunt's for the weekend, because my cousins, sisters and I would play in these same neighborhoods you see on Mini-Series, like "The Corner" and "The Wire". The same run down, drug infested, and boarded-up homes you see today in Baltimore City. Now don't get me wrong there was still crime and drugs in Baltimore in the 70's, but as a kid, my cousins, sisters and I, along with some neighborhood kids, all we wanted to do was play. And play we did. Games like: Red Light Green Light, Hot Butter Bean, Marbles, Scelly, and Hide and Go Seek. The girls played Jump Rope/Double Dutch, Jacks, and Bat and Ball. The boys played Basketball, not on a regular court with a goal, but with a milk cart tied or nailed to a street pole. Those were the days.

I also made a few friends with kids in my own neighborhood. We would love to walk to the mom-and-pop store for my mother, or just to buy junk like: Now and Laters, Boston Bake Beans, Chick O Sticks, etc. Now, the funny thing is some of these guys would go to the store with no money but come out with more junk than me. (lol). One of the kids looked at me crazy one day and said, "You never shoplift?" He stared at me like it was something all teens do. I said, "I don't know what kind of parents you have, but if my mom caught me stealing, she would break out the big belt for my butt." He said,

"Wow! You get beatens?" I said, "I haven't been in a while, but if my mom thought me or my sisters were out of line, a little pop in the butt will bring us back straight." He swears he will never get caught, but I'm not willing to take that chance. Anyway, my stepdad gives us little allowances from time to time, so there was no need to steal.

Crazy thing is, around June 1978 some of the criminal element in the neighborhood knew my stepfather was an MTA police officer. One day, while my family was out to dinner, someone broke into our home and stole my stepdad's 38 revolver. And they took nothing else, but that. Really sad. Hard to sleep at night, knowing your house has been violated and someone's out there with a gun. Well my stepdad wasn't having it and said that the neighborhood was changing from good to somewhat bad.

People started putting more locks on doors, putting extra bars on the windows, buying super screen doors with locks, and then buying the best protection out there - a German Shepherd dog. We had one, and of course his name was King. Around July of that year I started seeing mom and stepdad bringing home cardboard boxes from work. And surprisingly, we started packing up everything in our home. And in late July, we were out. It felt like the Jefferson's moving on up, only we were moving to the Northwest side of Baltimore.

Northwest Baltimore City. We moved to a nice middle-class community. The three major roadways that ran through my community were Wabash Ave, Reisterstown Rd., and Park Heights

Ave. We moved to a small community called Grove Park, which is closer to Wabash Avenue. What I quickly discovered that Wabash Ave, Reisterstown Rd., and Park Heights Ave. was crossed by Northern Parkway. So, you have one half of Northern Parkway, an African American community; and the other half, a Jewish community. And still, to this day, nothing has changed.

We moved in a neighborhood of semi-detached homes with driveways. A lot different from I'll old neighborhood a row homes. It was a three-bedroom home with a finished basement. It had a nice backyard and we hosted a lot of family cookouts, as the years went on. My first encounter of the neighborhood kids was my next-door neighbor, Eric. He was just a year younger than I, but he gave me a friendly run-down of the neighborhood teens. He asked me what grade I was going to. I replied the eighth grade. Now, I thought because of where we lived, that I will be going to Pimlico Junior High School. But no, he explained. Since we live in zone 15, I will be going to Fallstaff Middle, which had students from the 6th to 8th grades.

Wow, I would be going to this school for one year and then Northwestern High School, which is down the street from Fallstaff. Sounds good. A new teen to the neighborhood, especially a quiet and shy one like me, wanted to get outside more and make new friends; so during that summer, Eric introduced me to some of the other teens in the neighborhood (like Ricky, Kevin aka KC, Charles aka Chucky, Keith, Dennard, Kevin and Bryan C, Darryl, Lamont, Dana, Joey,

Finney, Steve, and my seems-like brother, Brian); and to this day, 38 years later, most of us are still close friends.

Junior high school and high school at Northwestern Senior High School were good times. As a Mid-teenager, I started to hear or learn the stereotypes that I hate today. Now, one of the first stereotypes you hear in an African American community is that black males raised in a two-parent household are likely to succeed, compared to black males raised in a single-parent household. I would be a fool to say, that in a single-parent household, the mom or dad cannot raise a successful man in the 80s, back then...or even now. I feel the difference from then and now, is there were more two-parent households back then. What happened to our communities?

Next stereotype, Black males are lazy. Negative. If you weren't going to summer camp, you had some sort of summer job or found a way to make extra money legally. Like cutting grass, or in the winter, shoveling snow. One of my first jobs, as a teenager, was at Sparkle Car Wash on Reisterstown Road. It was minimum-wage, but some of my friends and I received tips from each car we towel-dried. Now thinking back, one thing I wasn't taught, as a young man, was to save and invest my money. When we got paid, it was straight to the arcade. Not being taught this life-lesson of save, save, save and invest, will haunt me later.

A transition of decades from the 70s to the 80s was bringing a major change in the youth, and that was the music. The 80s was the beginning era of Rap music. Back in the day when I started to listen to Rap music, I called it feel good Rap. People today call it old school hip hop or classical, because it's still around. I came up in an Era where rap music was dance music, and most rappers had a story to tell. The Sugar Hill Gang in Rappers Delight. Everyone loved the samples of tracks from Old School Music; your parents danced too. Now it's remixed, and rappers put rhymes to it. Then suddenly, rap music went left (lol). There was a song, "The Genius of Love." Great song. But there was a verse in the song that seemed to be some guys in my neighborhood's favorite part. "What you going to do when you get out of jail? I'm going to have some fun." My thought was, *wait a minute you plan on going to jail?* (lol).

Rap music had to survive. So, I feel marketing teams look for ways to commercialize it, with shows on MTV called "Yo MTV Raps". Rap music started wars between the youth in some sense. But, no killings yet. The battles were breakdancing, or your crew versus my crew; also, rappers battled each other with their lyrics. One of my favorites was LL Cool J versus Kool Moe Dee. Classic. Then still great, rap went a little political; groups like Public Enemy, Boogie down Productions, KRS One, were my favorites. Fight the power that be. Now something like us fighting, the power they wanted to keep was dancing. Welcome, MC Hammer. You can't touch this. Then all of a sudden, out of nowhere.

Rap took a major turn. I feel, to be honest, a turn that affected the black community till this day. That turn was Gangsta Rap. I feel

Gangsta Rap music influenced some black young men to want to be a gangsta. But it wasn't supposed to be that way. Gangsta Rap gave the rappers or artists a voice to what was going on in their communities. Problem is some males, not all were trying to live what the media was betraying that gangsta rap was all about. I remember how kids from the one neighborhood wanted to fight kids from another neighborhood.

Yeah, they thought they had to protect a hood; yes, it was stupid, but the worse you got was a broken arm, maybe even a black eye… but you lived. You are probably good friends, afterwards. But I hate to say it gangsta rap evolved. It went from street fights to kids bringing guns to school. I remember my last year of high school. There were some kids going out front of Northwestern. In a split second, Pow! A gun went off and black youth laid dead. Why why why?

After high school it was my choice to join the military. And at only 17 years old, off to the Army I went. (Being all I can be). One thing for sure, and two things for certain, the military will make a man out of you really quick. Both physically and mentally. No doubt my upbringing, as a child, I was raised to do the right thing and make sound decisions. But the military taught me to be strong. There were trainings where you would push to the limit with your drill sergeant yelling in your ear, "If you're a quitter get out of my Army". Quitting was not an option for me, so I got focused and got through it.

The military teaches you to work with others. No matter one's color or religion. If one falls, pick him up and keep it moving. I, for the most part, always have respect for my elders. That's the way I was raised, so that laid the groundwork to respect the chain of command; from sergeants to generals. My years and the Army went by okay. I got to see different areas of the states, like Kentucky and Colorado. And I also had a one-year tour in Germany. Now, just like any other job, there were good days and bad. I served as an Armor Crewman a.k.a. a tanker.

There were days, during field training, when we had to train for days in the cold winters of Germany's country-sides and you would pray that the heater in your tank would last throughout the training (lol). While doing field training we had to eat prepackaged meals and drink warm coffee. Not to mention sharing a four-crewman tank with men who had not showered for days. But we were soldiers. And as I mentioned before, in order to survive the duties of the military, everyone got along.

Whether you are White, Black Asian or Latino, we rarely had no issues of where we were from or what was our skin color. I started to embrace different cultures and genres of music. Of course, I still listen to my R&B and rap. But I started liking and listening to country, pop, and rock 'n roll. The Rolling Stones, Quiet Riot, and AC/DC were my favorites.

My time in the military was only three years. Back in 1983, when I first enlisted, that was all the time you had to do unless you re-enlisted. Then, I think in 1985, it was changed to a mandatory four years of enlistment, instead of three. But in 1986, I had no plans or way reenlisting, it was time to go. Honorable discharge is how I left the military, with a couple of service pins, like sharpshooter, pinned to my uniform. Now it was time to get back to the streets of Baltimore Maryland USA and seek out my career path. God only knew what that would be.

CHAPTER TWO

ROOKIE YEARS

1987 fresh out of the military as a grown man, in time to pursue my career. I say career, but all I was getting was jobs (lol). One of my first jobs was at Maryland Nuts and Bolts Company. I was taught how to make and shape nuts and bolts from a steel rods. The steel rods had to be cut, bent and shaped in these hot pits of fire, then put into these machines to be shaped into your common nuts and bolts.

Working here required you to work in very hot conditions. In the summer time, it had to be over a hundred degrees, working in that hot box of a place. Needless to say, I didn't stay there too long; and my next adventure I remember was trying to sell vacuum cleaners. I would knock on people's doors with a fruit basket in hand, saying "did you get your free fruit basket today?" (lol). The customer would say 'what's the catch". You allow me to come in your home, vacuum and shampoo one room in your home for free. The customer would say," so a free vacuum and shampoo of one room and a free fruit basket, come on in. And the demonstration began. Will after an hour of work trying to show how great this vacuum/shampoo was? ...and it was okay. But convincing the customer about/the price of it, was the challenge.

Even the supervisor would come in with their little spiel was the routine. I think, out of every five demonstrations that were performed, I sold one (lol). So, door-to-door salesman was not my cup of tea. The next job I had was working at Domino's Pizza. Not the store that actually sells the pizza pies, but the factory that makes the dough that's put in crates and shipped to the stores. I think today is why Domino's is one of my favorite pizzas, because I know the dough is handmade fresh daily. Well, making dough wasn't the greatest job, but it was work.

This was the mid-80s, early 90s, and most of my friends were doing the same thing I was doing, finalizing their military career, finishing college, and looking for jobs and careers. As for me, I was trying to figure out what was my next move. I was doing what young males do, like dating multiple women without settling down. Never claim to be perfect.

As I think back, not too proud of myself, but I was young and young-minded. I've never been one for drugs; I'll just say I may have tried marijuana, weed, and pot, or whatever you wanna call it. And each time, it made me very paranoid or gave me the mindset of, *why do people get hooked on this? But who am I to judge?* Growing up in Baltimore, yes, I have friends who wanted to do things with their life; but also new guys in my neighborhood who sold drugs would be a means of income and they took drugs as well. Being a true, to what they call, product of your environment. Staying true to the so-called or thug life.

There were guys who I knew very well, carrying guns as a means of protection. Call me naïve, but it wasn't that serious. I know people who shot and killed a person over God knows what. And received a life sentence for murder. It wasn't new to hear black men being locked up for crimes that were due to what they considered being disrespected in the hood. You can't make this stuff up. You can see it in movies like "Boys n the Hood", but to witness it at the same time was a life experience. I normally have never been one to stay on a job long, so my venture of making dough was over. In my life I always gave advice to never leave a job unless you got another one lined up. I didn't follow my own advice and quit. Why did I do that? Finding another job was hard. So, I started working with the temp agency who was sending me out on little assignments. Some would be for days and some lasted for months.

My means of making money was low. They normally would send me two minimum wage jobs in factories and offices. I was 25 years old, and as a man, I realized I had to do better in my job choices. At one point, I was tempted with the drug-selling game, but I knew it wasn't an option. There were guys I knew that were in the game; you would see them with their nice cars, clothes, jewelry and pretty girls; but then you see the other part of the game, and that was going to jail or killed in some senseless murder. Nope, not about that life (lol). So, minimum wage jobs weren't the greatest, but I had my sanity. My temp agency landed me a job for the state of Maryland, as an office clerk for the Assessments and Taxation's Department. Not a great job for a young black male, but it got me an honest check once a week.

As an office clerk, working in this department, I was sorting and filing tax returns for businesses in the state of Maryland. Working in a business type atmosphere gave me a new perspective of Job versus the Corner (selling drugs). Here are people coming to work making good salaries, and their business attire, having some say this is the American dream. Me, on the other hand, living check to check. I didn't have to wear a suit for work and a businesslike atmosphere, I always owned at least more slacks, a dress shirt and loafers. There was a diverse group of people who worked in this office. For the most part, everyone was nice and gave me a good description of how the Tax and Assessment office works.

While I was there, if I had a college degree, I could have been hired for a full-time job, with the referrals from the staff working in the office. Good friendships were made, but I didn't have that degree. A couple people tried to encourage me to start taking college courses and even at 26 I wasn't too old to pursue a college degree. It's never too late to go back to school is what I heard a lot. But for me school was not my thing I also knew I can't do this clerk job forever. Being I worked in the state office building, the office for State of Maryland Employment was downstairs from where I worked. So, every now and then on my lunch break, I would go look at the job announcements to see if anything caught my eye or that I was qualified to apply for.

Hmm this is interesting. A posting for Correctional Officer Trainee. And it looks like I meet all the requirements. This looks interesting, so, I applied. Kind of excited, I got together all the documents I needed like: high school diploma, army's proof of military time, and job references. I filled out the application and turned everything in a few days later. About a month or two later, I was called in for a physical and a drug test. Past that, of course, (lol). And then it happened, I called a couple weeks later to check on the status of my application. The response I got back made my day. Mr. Bryant, you are hired, you should be getting an acceptance letter in a couple of days starting as a correctional officer at the Maryland Reception Diagnostics and Classification Center a.k.a. MRDCC.

August 4, 1993 I was excited and nervous at the same time. This was the first day of my correctional career. Starting as a rookie is not the greatest salary in the world, but it was a career where I had unions and medical benefits if I got sick, needed dental work, or eyeglasses. It was a career that had a 401K plan and a retirement plan, that if I stayed 20 years I can collect a pension. I say again, the salary was okay not great; but officers supplemented the okay salary by working overtime a.k.a. OT. But I was new to corrections and I wanted to learn the job first, before I started working OT.

My first day on the job was just like any other new job and it was a bunch of filling out paperwork, tax forms, and signing up for medical insurance. Next, it was classes on pretty much what to be expected of a correctional officer. Day two was getting uniforms and a class on the gun range. The range is where we went on a third day to qualify on the revolver and shotgun that is used, in corrections.

Sometimes inmates go out of these institutions. Hospitals, court, or just moving from one facility to another, officers must be trained, qualified, and ready with these weapons, in case the inmates tries to escape under your custody. My military training gave me the skills I needed to do well at the range. Now there were some offices who never held a weapon before in their life, but if you listened to the instructors and get over your initial fear of pulling that shotgun trigger and feeling that kick and hearing that boom; even the beginners of weapons' virgins will do fine. That thing was (back then) you had to qualify with a certain score or you were dismissed of having this job. So back then, every officer had to pass or you'll be looking for a job elsewhere.

Fast-forward to now will only select officers that qualify yearly with the weapons. You don't go three days, after getting hired, in which it was mandatory to pass. But now, if you're lucky, you may go a year after working in corrections; or if you show interest in working on outside duties, like transporting inmates to court, hospital, or various institutions in the state. I figured it was a way to save the state money. The less officers you have, good qualifiers, the less money you spend on teaching officers how to shoot. Those practice bullets cost money (lol). Anyway, back to the past. If you pass the range, the fourth day is when it gets real. After receiving your uniform, the previous days, you must go out and get it altered and go out to buy black boots; because, on the fourth day, we did tours, and were assigned to monitor officers throughout the facility. I think this was a ploy to see if you really wanted to work there. They took us on tour throughout the facility Thursday and Friday, so you could get a feel on what you got yourself into.

The five-week training Academy starts on Monday, but if you were shook up from the correctional scene from last Thursday and Friday you'll have second thoughts about going to the Academy on Monday. With the guidance of the training Sgt. or veteran officer, they took the group of new officers, which included me through the various parts of the institution. First stop, we met with the warden of the institution. He or she is a top person in charge to make sure the institution is running under the state standards, and everyone is following policies and procedures of the institution.

Of course, we got the welcome aboard speech and away we went. We left there to go into the actual core of the institution. We went through some doors, which led us to some elevators. We rode the elevator up a floor and got off; instantly, I felt like a deer or gazelle, because there was a holding cell of inmates looking like lions focusing on their prey. Your first thought was to say, "What the hell are y'all looking at?" But it was my first week on the job, so I better keep it professional. We went to the receiving /intake/release area. The officers working there explain the process of working in this area. Then it was lunch time for us, so we went to eat in the officers' dining room a.k.a. ODR. Not too appetizing, at first, especially when you find out the inmates or trustees make and prepare your food.

Now, they are supervised by dietary officers; but it is just the thought of it all. Next, we visited the medical department. Now get this: inmates or arrestees - whatever you want to call them - get free medical, dental, and prescription medication. Well free to them, but a course, it is a taxpayer's nightmare. Unless your job pays for getting this kind of medical insurance, it is expensive, and you'll still pay for some kind of way with deductibles and co-pays. And here the inmates, because he or she is locked up in a state prison getting better health coverage than senior citizens out here struggling just to get Medicaid. Only in America (lol.) Next stop is a regular housing unit. As soon as we walked in, just like downstairs, all the inmates came to the cell doors - 32 cells in total, which means 64 inmates to a housing unit.

The crazy thing, is I only see one officer working in the unit. So that's a 64 to 1 inmate, two-officer ratio. Let's think about this for moment. Mixed in this housing unit, you have murderers, rapists, robbers, pedophiles, arsonists, drug users, drug dealers, gang members, thieves; and let's not forget the white-collar crimes - tax evaders and money launderers. Also, you have the percentage who say they were falsely accused of a crime and they have no idea why they are there;

"seriously?" is what I say (lol). Oh yeah, I can't forget the ones who were at the wrong place at the wrong time; but being they don't want to snitch on the person who had actually done the crime, they decided to take the charge and the jail-time that came with it. So, you have this big mixing pot of 64 inmates, with one officer in a housing unit. Another thing I must mention is, as much as society and the media have people believe, these are not all black men or youth. I can tell you firsthand, after looking at the ID board, where all the inmates' IDs are kept while on the housing units.

There is every race and skin color locked up in this prison and all prisons. Crime has no particular color. All training Sgt. /tour guides asked was, "Do we have any questions for the housing unit officer? Will the group of new officers and I, ask what I think are standard new officer questions? Have you ever been in or seen fights?" "No," the officer replied. "I have never been in a fight, but that's not to say officers can't get assaulted by these inmates. Some inmates will respect you and some have nothing to lose. It could be some kind of gang initiation, so they will start a fight with an officer just to prove they are tough to the other inmates."

So, once again, always be aware. As for them fighting each other, that's common, so be aware. Remember, react, and call the code on your radio for "inmates fighting". That will give some help to you; never attempt to break up a fight by yourself. What are your work hours? The work hours here are as follows 7-3, 3-11, 11-7 shifts. If one particular shift is short, officers can get what's called drafted, and they would have to work the next shift. So always have a plan B if you have kids to pick up from daycare. Also, you can volunteer to work overtime.

Do the inmates give you problems? Some inmates will give you respect and then there are some who try you to see what they can get away with. For me, I say no to most of their questions, that way they know not to ask me for anything (lol). What's the ID board for? The ID board is for accountability. If the inmate leaves the housing unit on a pass, let's say to the medical unit they carry their IDs. That way it gives us a quick reference of whose out, who's in. But word of advice, when it comes to count time, don't go by the ID board, physically go around cell to cell and count bodies. You may think someone is out, but he's actually in the cell with his ID in his pocket.

Working here is not as bad as one may think, you have good days, and you have bad days. It's all about how you handle situations and react to them. My duties include following policies and procedures of the institution (textbook answer). Custody and security, making sure the inmates are not harming each other or the staff. Always, I repeat, always, pay attention to what's going on in your house unit. These guys come out the cells to go on pass throughout the institution, for showers, for recreation and phone calls, and to eat. So, paying close attention to what's going on in your housing unit is important. Other than that, ask questions, be yourself, and learn all you can at the Academy. Good luck. Well that was interesting. That moment in the housing unit gave us some insight on what we will be doing on a daily basis.

Our next stop was the segregation unit. It is where the institution houses inmates, who are on disciplinary custody (they were fighting, or damaged state property), protective custody (kept separate based on their charges), and administration custody (kept separate by the institution from general population). The inmates called this housing unit jail, within jail. The setup is the same as the previous housing unit we were in… just smaller. The segregation unit officers gave us insight of this segregation unit. First of all, there are two offices working here, compared to one officer working in general population units. They both wore protective stab vests.

There were only 16 cells here, compared to 32 cells in the other housing unit. These inmates are in a single cell compared to two in the cell and the other housing units. Every time an inmate comes out in the segregation unit, they are handcuffed for the officers and staff safety. They come out for just one hour a day and shower. When his time is to be fed, their food is taken to them, and we give it to them through a slot in the door. Compared to the other house units where the inmates come out of their cells to get their trays of food. This is a very sensitive unit to work; and some say this is where you'll find you're most disruptive and notorious inmates housed. Being these are single man cells, some inmates in other parts of the institution may start a fight with staff or other inmates, just because they know they will be brought here to this housing unit for being disruptive.

Some inmates don't care that they are locked in a cell, 23 hours a day, they don't care that they shower every other day, and they don't care that their food is fed to them through a slot. All they care about is they have that extra protection of not being around general population inmates in the yards or day room. They get a single cell where they can sleep in peace and not worry about their cellmate jumping on you in the middle of the night, or your cellmate stealing your commissary (food, snacks, and hygiene products). And you can take a pee or poop in peace and not worry about your cellmate smelling or seeing you. In their minds, it's a little price to pay for peace of mind.

Our last stop - the classification area. This area is where many inmates come on a pass to meet with their parole agent or classification counselor. We met with a classification counselor who gave us a brief description on what they do. We meet with the inmates that come into the institution. And based on a point system that we use, determine where they may do their incarceration time. You get points on the type of crime committed: Is this your first time being locked up? What was your life like before you got locked up? (Like where were you working?), and other various questions. All this determines your security level.

Being pre-released the lowest, minimum, medium, and maximum the highest. And here in Maryland, we have certain correctional institutions for each level of inmates. That being said, these inmates here at MRDCC are not housed here long. Once they get their medical assessment done, and classification done, they are shipped to an institution here in Maryland, where they would do their incarceration time. So, ideally, they are only here maybe 90 days, if everything goes as planned.

Okay, the first week of being a trainee is over; but it's the weekend and it gives you a lot of things to think about for you attend the Academy Monday morning. Yes, one has applied and gotten the job to work in Maryland Correction. For all you have seen and all the officers you talk to, definitely have to be mentally prepared, and maybe a little psycho (lol) to work in corrections. Working as a correctional officer is not for everyone. I didn't fully understand what that meant, at first, but over the years it became clear.

Bright and early Monday morning I was there at the Academy, eager and ready to learn. As I looked around the room I spotted the other officers that were from my institution (MRDCC) that I started with. It was good to see no one backed out. From what we saw, the previous week at the institution; "saying Dam that Job" (lol). Looking around the room, I'm guessing we have 60 to 70 new trainees from various correctional institutions in Maryland. A rough guess, out of the 70, at least 40 males.

There's a reason I mentioned this, which will be addressed later in this book. But anyway, the class began. The instructors came in and introduced themselves in the classes they were going to teach. Just off, first impression, we had a feeling of the instructors who would keep our attention, and the ones you'll be fighting yourself to stay awake. Some of the classes involved were Emergency Plans (in case of any emergency, riot, fire, escape, etc.) Use of force (how to handle disruptive inmates), First Aid and CPR (in case you had to save a life); and, of course, restraint classes, teach you how to properly put restraints on an inmate.

Then there was a small boring class that they usually gave after lunch, so It was a struggle to keep your eyes open (lol). The Academy was about 4 to 5 weeks, in which, at the end we had OC Spray and Mace class. We had to go through a gas chamber with gas masks on; but once we were in, we had to take them off for a moment to get the effects of OC Spray or Mace, if it was sprayed in an area. Being I had a similar training in the Army, I had an idea of the effects of this gas. But the people who never smelled the stuff before, got a rude awakening. The coughing, vomiting, teary eyes, and burning skin didn't make for a fun day. But, we all got through it.

From weeks one through five at the Academy you started to build bonds and work together with people you just met for the first time. You would make new friends and attempt to keep in touch, once the Academy is over. We started out with about 70 trainees, but we lost about six for various reasons - like failing tests, too many lateness, or just having the fear of working in the jails. Once again, this job is not for everyone. Graduation day, we had our pot luck feast. We congratulated each other for making it through.

Our certified correctional officer certification certificates were distributed. And the top students received special certificates for honorable students. You had to have no demerits, never late or absent, and at least 95% on all your tests. I almost got it, but I received a demerit for shaking the candy machine during a lunch. Hey, what can I say, my chips got stuck and didn't fall. I had a sense of accomplishment. Kind of like when I graduated from high school or finishing basic training in the military. But talking and listening to my fellow trainee officers, "The real training starts Monday when we're back."

Chapter Three

Here We Go

The weekend. Time to relax and try not to think about my first official day as a correctional officer when I return to MRDCC on Monday morning. After you graduate from the Academy, your first year as officer you're on a probationary period. Yup, 12 months to see if you are really cut out for this type of work. I think it only takes a week, the things you see in jail. But your supervisors - Lieutenants and Captains - want to make sure you can follow policies and procedures, you can maintain a professional attitude in certain situations and; of course, just like any other job, you can report to work on time and not call out, unless it's an emergency. So yes, you may have graduated from the Academy with honors; that doesn't mean what you learned in the Academy, you can put that knowledge into a working correctional environment. So, I try not to think about Monday, and focus on the weekend.

My friend/brother Brian and I shared what I called a single man's bachelor apartment. We lived in Randallstown Maryland. And when the time presented itself, we partied. Friends I grew up with from the old neighborhood like Ricky, K C, Chucky, and a few others would come over to hang out, get some drinks, and play cards. And being that we were all single, women would love to come and hang out... and the party was on. Our apartment was live on the weekend! But this weekend, for me, there was no heavy drinking. Maybe a beer or two to toast my accomplishment of finishing the Academy. But I wanted to stay focused and have my mind clear of the new world of corrections that I had to face on Monday morning. So, no hangovers on my first day.

Monday morning, I arrived like a new officer would, at 6:20 AM (the shift started at 7 AM); with my uniform pressed, brass shined, shoes polished and a fresh haircut. I felt really sharp. Also, my fellow new trainees, whom I was in the Academy with, were pretty much looking the same way, clean. Once we entered the building, we were given instructions to go to the Roll Call room and meet with the training Sgt., after Roll Call for further instructions.

The Roll Call happened at the beginning of all three shifts (7am–3pm, 3pm-11pm, and 11pm-7am). It was given by the shift supervisors (Majors, Captains and Lieutenants), for accountability of the officers, making sure everyone reported to work on time; for information from previous shifts, like were there any fights or assaults, and to give officers their work assignments for that day. Now as my fellow trainees and I were sitting there, I noticed some of the officers that were coming into the room. Maybe it's because I am a new officer, but some (not all) of these officers' uniforms looked terrible (lol). They were not pressed, at all. They had the look of when someone washed their clothes, left them in the dryer for hours before taking them out, wrinkle city. *Well, instead of using an iron, I'll just put these on.*

I know I'm a rookie, but damn, take some pride in your uniform. Next thing I noticed was that Roll Call started at 6:48 AM. Once again, I know I am a rookie, so being on time (early) is expected of me; but there were officers coming in at 6:46 /6:47 and running in at 6:48. OK! Now that's pushing it (lol). But anyway, that was my first Roll Call. After Roll all, all the officers filtered out of the room to their posts. The new officers and I were left behind to meet with the shift Lieut. and training Sgt.

We were told for the next three days that we will be observing veteran officers on how housing units are run. Two days of just watching and learning, and, on the third day, the veteran officers will observe us running the housing unit like we were on our own. We were also told that the 7 to 3 shift will not be our permanent shift. And on the fourth day, some of us will go to the 3 to 11 shift, and some of us will go to the 11 to 7 shift. I was thinking to myself that sucks because I never work any evening shifts. And as it turned out, I was going to the 3 to 11 shift.

We were given calendars on how our days off went. And we were given instructions on what to do if we needed a day off. We were told vacations will be hard to get, being that we were the lowest on the totem pole. So, after that brief discussion with the Lieut. and Sgt. we were off to our prospective housing units. Here We Go!

The way this institution is set up elevators take you to your prospective floor. Seven floors in all, and a basement where the dietary, and the storeroom and maintenance were. We all, of course, went to different places; but every time one of us got off the elevator on different floors, we would say "good luck", and see you at the end of the shift. I don't remember where my first housing unit was, but it was a regular housing unit. Getting off the elevator, you were greeted by an officer who worked in the corridor or hallway and they let you into one of the housing units. And as I mentioned earlier, each unit held 64 inmates, except the segregation unit, which held 16. The corridor officer asked me, "Are you a new officer?" And I replied, "Yes. I'm Officer Bryant and I'm going to one of the housing units." That was 22 years ago so I forgot which one was my first (lol). What I do remember, like it was yesterday is that the officer opened the door of the housing unit and I walked in.

The housing unit officer was letting inmates out of their cells. I'm assuming to go out on passes throughout the institution. Once they were finished, she came down and introduced herself, and I did as well. Once all the inmates were ready to go out, she began to search them for contraband. It's called a pat search, where you just search the outer garments of a person's body, trying to find contraband like knives, shanks, drugs, and cell phones. The inmates were handed their passes and IDs, and out the door they went. After that, the officer and I had some small talk about the job and what her day consisted of. I remember one of the first things the officer told me was, whatever I learned in the Academy forget about it.

With a confused look on my face I said, "What! She said, "Let me explain. Yes, the Academy teaches you the basics, but when you're actually doing the job is when you learn more. When you're actually doing counts and the inmates are actually in their cells, is when you learn. When you have to break up fights or call staff assaults on the radio is when you're really training. The next real and valuable thing I can tell you is, don't try to take shortcuts. Veteran officers, who have been here for a while, take shortcuts. One example is, let's say it's time to feed them; you're only supposed to open no more than four cells at a time. That's eight inmates that will come out to eat. But some officers will open eight cells at a time trying to finish fast; now that can be a problem. If a fight breaks out and you have sixteen inmates out instead of eight; how do you explain that to the Lieut. who has to investigate the incident.

The next piece of advice that I will give you is be yourself. If you weren't Superman on the streets, don't come in here acting like Superman. Oh yeah, another thing is keep your home business to yourself. Inmates don't need to know your information, like where you live, how many kids you got, what you do when you get off work, things of that nature. And this place is like a soap opera. Officers don't have nothing better to do but to smile in your face and talk and spread rumors behind your back." Well, I said, "I don't remember none of these classes in the Academy."

The rest of our day went on. We let out inmates for their recreation. They watched TV and played cards and sat around and talked (probably plotting and scheming their escape here). After recreation was over we locked them in and it was time for their lunch. "Feed Up", is what we called it. Four cells at a time came down, got their meal, and went back to their cell. Once again, I can't remember exactly what the meal was, but I do remember the dessert was cookies, and we had enough cookies for 28 cells. Four cells did not get cookies with their meal and they were like kids who were told they couldn't have any candy. The officer had to call downstairs to the dietary department and have the dietary staff send up cookies for eight inmates. Funny thing is, the inmates waited at their cell doors - looking like kids staring at the chimney waiting for Santa to come down - waiting on these cookies.

Another quick rule I learned, always, I say again, always count your food and utensils before you start feeding. Because the dietary department would swear they sent you the right amount of food. *Life lessons of corrections.* After feeding the inmates, we were relieved by another officer for our lunch break. The famous officer dining room, or in short, ODR. For your dining pleasure. If you say your prayers for your meals, this was the time to do it. Some things are edible, and some things, you're really taking a chance with. And if all else fails, there are vending machines for snacks and sodas. But you can't count on eating junk food, every day for lunch. You'll be gaining a lot of weight if you do that. So, you just had to pick and choose what you were going to eat from the ODR.

After lunch we returned to our housing unit to proceed with the rest of our day. It was one of the most important parts of the day. Count Time! Count Time! Make sure every inmate hears you, loud and clear. We walked around to each cell with a count sheet and clipboard. If the inmate was in we put a check on the count sheet; if he was out we put his name, inmate number, and where he was out to, in the appropriate box. Your ins and outs had to equal up to the number of inmates that were in your housing unit. The veteran officer stressed that this was another shortcut veteran officers fail on. Instead of actually getting up and going door to door, making sure they see two living breathing inmates in each cell, they used the ID board and tried to count IDs instead of bodies.

Now, who's to say the inmate came back from their pass and didn't give you his ID. Count Time. You see a missing ID and assume he's still out, but actually he's in his cell eating Little Debbie snacks he received from commissary. (Commissary: when your loved ones send you money and you able to buy hygiene products, writing material, stamps, finger foods and snacks). Anyway, this mishap on your part, by not getting up and counting bodies can hold up the total institutional count. Which can cause a recount.

The first thing on an institutional recount, you're thinking to yourself, *did someone escape?* But the truth is someone in the institution miscounted, and you just hope it wasn't you. Turning in a wrong count can lead to some sort of a reprimand from your supervisors. So, the bottom line is to just get up and do it the right way. Once the count was clear and all the inmates in the institution were accounted for, we sent a few more inmates out on passes. Some were going to the pack-up unit. This was a unit where the officers working there inventoried and packed up all your property, because you were leaving to go to another institution in Maryland, where you'll be doing your actual time that you were sentenced to.

The correctional institution security levels go as follows: Pre-release institutions house inmates with probably less than a year. Institutions with a minimum-security level, house inmates with a little over a year. Institutions with a medium security level may house inmates with 3 to 5 years. Maximum security level institutions, based on your crime, may house inmates from five years to life. Then there are Super Max, these institutions house inmates with life and high-profile crimes. If you're in a Super Max institution, you're pretty much on death row; and nine times out of ten, unless the governor calls, you're not getting out.

The rest of the passes consisted of medical, parole agents, public defenders, and of course, visits. The inmate's family, friends, wife, baby mothers - as they say, come to the institution to pay a visit to these guys. The inmate fills out a visiting card of all the people they want to visit them. If you're not on the visiting card, you can't visit - sorry, I guess he forgot about you. The crazy thing with this is, some guys will put their wife, girlfriend, and baby mother on the same visiting card. So, there were some instances, where at least two would show up at the same time. That got a little ugly in the visiting room.

Little female cat fights happen, every now and then. Well, after all that it was 3 o'clock, and that was the end of our day.

Now on the outside looking in, that didn't seem like a bad day. But as a correctional officer, that can be a very stressful day. Sometimes, it could be that one little thing that would turn your whole day around. You may ask for an example, okay he is a few of many (lol). Some inmates will ask you a question. You will give them the most correct and truthful answer as possible, but being it is not what they want to hear, they will request and want you to call your supervisor Lieut. You tell them they will be in here making rounds, sometime during the shift, but to them, that's not fast enough; so, they scream out the cell and bang on a door. Maybe even using toilet paper or a washcloth to stop up the toilet or sink causing a flood, just to get some attention. Then the Sgt. or the lieutenants will come to see what is going on. Now this is the part that pisses you off.

The lieutenant comes and asks the inmate what is going on, why did you flood the unit, or why are you kicking in the door. The inmate responds with the same question he asked you earlier, hoping he gets a different response. But when the lieutenant gives him the same answer you gave him earlier, he gets humble and apologizes for him yelling and kicking the door. It makes you want to say to him *isn't that what the Fuck I told you earlier*. But we're4 not supposed to curse to the inmates (lol). Another thing that will give you a bad day is we're not psychiatrists. So, we as correction officers, don't know what an inmate is going through. In the Academy we get suicide prevention classes.

This class gives you the basic recognition of signs and symptoms of suicide prevention. But when you go to work and are making your rounds, you will hope the class prepared you enough, when you find an inmate tied his sheet around his neck and is attempting or successfully committed suicide. That will definitely give you a bad day. Another thing is C.O.'s are not doctors or nurses; but faithfully, every day, you will have someone banging on the door saying this. "C.O. I Got Chest Pains!" Once again, we're not medical professionals, so it is our duty to call the medical department to get him some medical attention. And nine times out of 10, that's all he wants is some attention. Screaming "chest pains!" gives them the opportunity to get out of the cell and take a trip to the medical department.

Once in the medical department, the nurses usually just take their vitals, maybe give them a heart scan and once it is determined that it is not a heart attack; but rather the food they ate fast, at lunch time, they send them right back to the housing unit. What makes the correctional officers a little upset is it's the same inmates all the time. Sometimes it gets so frustrating that some officers do what's called spinning the Inmate. Inmate: "C. O. I got chest pains!" Officer: "What's your name and what cell are you in?" Inmate: "My name is blah blah, and I'm in cell 5." Officer: "Okay, blah. I'm calling the medical unit right now."

Now, the officer does pick up the phone (lol), so the inmate can clearly see them, but they fake dial and act like they're talking to a nurse on the phone. Then they go to cell 5 and tell the inmate, "Blah, they said they're going to call for you; but is almost shift change, so you will go to medical on the next shift." Classic. The problem is the officer leaves, giving the next officer the problem, with inmate Blah Blah thinking he's going to medical.

Another problem that correctional officers go through is inmates who don't want to lock in their cells after recreation is over or coming back from a pass. They do this for various reasons (I think they forget they're in jail). But a reason can be they're being threatened, raped, or beat up by their cell mate. Or maybe other inmates in that housing unit are threatening them. So, not locking in is a good way to get written up and moved from that housing unit to the segregation unit. Inmates learn the tricks of the trade. And as correctional officers our hands are tied with some of this foolishness. These kinds of incidents happen on a normal day of a correctional officer's duty. We deal with it, but it stresses you out over a period of time and lets me remind you that these are just some of the things correctional officers go through.

My first day is over, and the next day is the same, observe and learn. On the third day, the veteran officer shadowed me, and I ran the housing unit like it was my own. The following week I went to my new shift, where they normally send new officers. The 3 to 11 shift. The first couple of days I had to learn how this shift's daily routine runs; it's a little different from the 7 to 3 shift. The first thing we did when we got to the unit was to give the inmates showers. The housing units had a top and a bottom level, 16 cells on each level, 64 inmates total.

The top and the bottom level, flip flop shower days. Which means inmates will get showers every other day. If it wasn't the inmates' shower day, they would usually take a birdbath in their cell sink. The life of being locked up. Anyway, we started the day off with showers. And with only four showers on the housing units, inmates got (get this) five-minute showers. Inmates, two cells at a time would go in the showers. Five minutes later, the officer would yell "time up in the showers". (That meant bring your butt out). Those four would come out and lock in, then the next four would go in.

Now if everything goes as planned, this should take about 45 minutes with the inmates going to and from their cells. But we are talking about inmates, with some who never had any respect for authority. Some would take 6 to 7 minutes, and you would have to yell," Get Out the Showers!" Some would walk so slow just taking their sweet ole time. Some just had to make a quick stop at their buddy's cell and you had to yell at them about that. So, a 40-minute job usually takes about an hour.

Our next duty is our first count. (Count Time, Count Time). Once that clears, the food cart arrives, and we do feed up. After feeding the inmates (you may get relieved for lunch during a time), it may be a good time to sort and pass out the mail. Between 5 and 6 o'clock the officers have a little free time to sit back and breathe, trying to clear your mind of the first half of the day; and repair yourself for the second half of the day, which consists of recreation.

On the 3 to 11 shift, the inmates (like Showers) flip-flop recreation days from top to bottom. So, from 6:30 p.m. to 9:30 p.m. you have 32 inmates out with you. Three hours of, "Keep the Noise Down, chasing guys off the phone, so the next guy can get on, inmates arguing over card games, and an occasional fight. The life of inmate recreation. After recreation is over at 9:30 PM you lock everyone in. Then we have inmate trustee workers, cleanup the housing unit or tier, by sweeping and mopping. They also clean up the showers, as well. Daily, at least 32 men have used the showers.

So, it's no telling what kind of germs, dirt, or fluids are on these shower floors. Can someone say, nasty! Between 9:45 – 10:00 p.m. we are doing another count. This count should clear around 10:30 PM. That gives you a half an hour before you get off at 11 PM, to sit back, take a breath, pray, and relax until you get off. Hopefully, and I do mean hopefully, you had a good day, without drama or incidents. The routine is pretty much the same every day. The time can be thrown off slightly due to a bad count or dietary running out of food for one of the housing units, and you have to wait for the food to arrive. Other than that, it's the same routine every day.

Officers change post every 60 days. This was good because it gives you a chance to see and work in different areas of the institution, and not see the same inmates, over and over again. The switching of officers every 60 days also was good because the inmates didn't get used to how one particular officer ran things. Inmates study officers. It's like they have nothing else better to do, but to watch you. To see how you react to certain things or situations. You hear it in the Academy and from veteran officers: always say no. If they ask can they pass something to the cell next to them, say no. Because if you let them pass little stuff, they expect for you to say yes to passing stuff all the time. And the stuff can be a shank or drugs that are hidden in a book. *Makes sense.*

The first days on one 3 to 11 shift, were like my first couple of days training on the 7 to 3 shift, observing the veteran officer and learning the routine. After that, I was on my own. This is where all I was taught and learned come into play. As I walked into my first housing unit (to work alone), once again all eyes were on me, or maybe it was not just me, but that's how I felt. But anyway, I received all my equipment (Radio, Handcuffs, Mace, and Keys) from the officer on the unit that had worked the previous shift. They relayed information from their shift and let me know about the inmates that were out on passes.

The officer gave me one last look and said, "are you good?" My response was, "yeah I guess". Their reply was, "well okay;" and out the door they went. As I signed into my logbook, I planned today's routine in my mind. Showers, count, eat/feed, an inmate recreation, count again, think, and then go to hell home. Once I was finished writing, I looked up, and out of 32 doors at least 25 had eyes looking up. Now I know how a lost gazelle feels walking into a den of lions. But I had to let them know I wasn't a gazelle; that I was a lion who grew up in the streets of Baltimore. So, I yelled out, "Bottom Tier, get ready for Showers!" And my career as a correctional officer officially begins.

For the next 3 to 4 years, I grow from a rookie in corrections to an eager, and willing-to-learn correctional officer. Soaking it all in, I experience and learn new things every day. One thing for sure, you can't get complacent. You've always got to be aware of what's going on around you. One day I remember, the top tier was out for recreation. Everything was going normal. The inmates, were doing their normal things of playing cards, making phone calls, and watching TV. After walking through the tier, chitchatting with the inmates, I went to my desk to write in my log book. Then all of a sudden, I hear some inmates yell out, "CO, this guy is having a seizure!" I go up to observe the situation (with caution, of course, because you never know with inmates) and on the floor lied an inmate, shaking.

I immediately called Medical Emergency on the radio and, within seconds, the shift sergeant, other officers, and some medical staff arrived. Then I yelled out to the inmates that were out to "stand by your cell doors!" The shift sergeant replied, don't lock the inmates in yet. The medical staff referenced to the Sgt. that the guy who had a seizure's lip looked busted. At that time, the Sgt. pulled me and a couple of other officers aside, and told us before we locked the inmates in their cells, that he needed to check for blood on their hands and clothes. And sure, enough one of the inmates met the description (blood on knuckles and T-shirt).

Come to find out, that inmate one hit inmate two so hard, it busted his lip and he fell into a seizure. Unbelievable, but true. Just in that split second, I had what I thought was a medical emergency, turned out to be an inmate-on-inmate assault. And I missed the whole thing. I felt kind of bad. But like I said, inmates watch you and as hard as you try, you can't keep your eyes on everything. And given any chance to fight, steal, or pass contraband, they'll seize the opportunity, when permitted. Yes, it is a challenge, but officers must be observant with these guys.

My downtime was "me" time. Working in corrections, your days off cannot come fast enough. Heck, I was in my 20s and single with a fairly good salary coming in bi-weekly. Was I saving and investing like I should've been doing? No! I was blowing my money on stupid material things, because that's all that seemed to matter. I'm not afraid to admit my mistakes in life, because, to me, I look at it as a learning experience; and in the future, I'll teach my children to do better in their life experiences and to make good decisions when they come of age. Blowing money and bad decisions is how I was living.

I'll share the time I came home to my apartment that I shared with one of my friends. I got home one night, after working my shift. I got to my apartment, put the key in the door and went in. *Oh, my goodness, where is my furniture! Hold up, am I in the right apartment?* The whole place was empty, and I'll remind you this was around 12 midnight. Now, of course, cell phones were not thought of then (just pagers and beepers), so I went out to the gas station across the street and used the payphone.

I called my mother's house and asked her," Have you heard from my friend Brian?" Her reply was, "yes he's right here." Brian got on the phone and said, "Man we got evicted!" (lol) It's funny now, but not back then. That's when I noticed a row of furniture and bags on the street in front of the apartment building. It looked like we weren't the only ones who got evicted that day. I just couldn't believe that this was some of our stuff. Brian mentioned he and some other friends grabbed some of our most important things, as much as they could. But when they came back to get some more stuff, the looters had gone through our things and stolen most of our belongings. Bastards!

Oh well, a life lesson... I went back home to my mom's. Embarrassed, of course. One of my sisters was looking at me with disbelief. She was rubbing it in with comments like, "that's all that partying you'll always doing every weekend" and "I bet you'll pay your bills on time the next time you move out." *What a life lesson.*

This was the mid to late 90s. In my life, I for the most part, try to stay positive, and look for the good in things. But the African American was still experiencing a lot of racial profiling. The Rodney King indictment, Wow! *Can't we just get along?* The O.J. Simpson case, trial, and verdict made America erupt. If you were a rap music fan you had the East Coast/West Coast feud. Biggie versus Tupac and Knight versus Puffy. Unbelievable. On top of all that you had a Gulf War going on. I remember having dreams of not completely finishing my military enlistment time and had to go fight in the Gulf Wars. *Nightmares indeed.* On the good note, we did have America Online (AOL), and the World Wide Web was booming.

My career with corrections was going pretty well. I vowed to try, I say again try, to manage my salary a little better. When I moved again, the last thing I wanted to do was get evicted. *Not a good feeling.* Being I was learning new areas of my correctional institution (MRDCC), I started working overtime just to make extra money and attempt to save. I've been in my mother's/stepfather's house for about eight months now, and for a man in his mid-20s I feel it is too old for a man to be in his parents' house. *I got to go.*

Well I got lucky. I, a cousin of mine, (William, who was a Baltimore City Police Officer) had an Apartment in Northwest Baltimore. He kind of was in the same boat I was in, wanting to get out of his Mom's house, but save money at the same time. He asked if I would be willing to help him share the rent and utilities at his place. I said, "no doubt." And for the fact I wanted to get out of my parents' home, I moved the next day. Being the apartment was in the city and I was still on the 3 to 11 shift, my commute to work was only 20 minutes.

Not bad, only problem is there were limited places to park when I got off of work.

After being there a couple of months, I remember one night when I got off work, with the limited parking, I had to park at the end of the parking lot in our apartment complex. Bad mistake. When I came out the next morning to move my car, my back window was smashed, the trunk was open, and the glove compartment was open. Some Dumb Ass Mutherfucker done broken into my car. Life in the city. I'm going to work and take it out on somebody. The first inmate that asks me a dumb ass question is probably going to get cursed out.

CHAPTER FOUR

SEE YOU UPTOWN

A merica has let Americans down. I say again, America has let Americans down. My conspiracy theory. Please don't call me crazy, hear me out. It's been said that some sort of Secret Societies hold these meetings of the minds. Their agenda. How to disrupt and corrupt a certain group of people. Now, I'm not going to pinpoint a race, ethnicity, or specify what group of people, just paint a picture. Now this group of people, (yes, they are Americans) live in some of the poorest and most rundown neighborhoods in some states in America.

The secret meeting begins. First let's find a way to take jobs out of these communities and move them to foreign countries. We will keep our large corporations, right in the heart of their downtown areas, but will make sure that most are not qualified to hold a position in that company. Let's find a way to take jobs out of these communities and move them to places that are not assessable to public transportation. Next, on the agenda, is to find a way to let the drug cartels and kingpins filter their drugs into these communities. Let some people in these communities sell drugs a.k.a. drug dealers for means of making money. Only push to incriminate the small-time drug dealers and their lookouts.

Next on the agenda. We need to find a way to mess with the goods and services. First, no one who lives in these communities can own any retail or grocery stores. The people who do own these stores, (foreigners) make them sell overpriced food and hygiene products. For example, a 12-ounce box of cereal will cost five-dollars in their community. But the same cereal, a 24-ounce box would only cost four-dollars in your Walmart's or Kmart's of the world. Oh yeah, keep the Walmart's and the Kmart's out of these communities, place them where limited public transportation goes.

Next on the agenda, let's put a liquor store every 2 to 3 blocks away. We'll find a way to make the wine and the beer prices cheap, we won't overprice the alcohol. Next, give business loans to the Chinese to sell their fried rice, give business loans to the Koreans for hair and nail shops, give business loans to the Arabs for convenience stores (yeah sell them Slurpees), more business loans to the Asians to sell overpriced D Batteries and chicken wings and fries. Well, what about African-American loans. Let's see, first only the real Africans from Africa; they can braid hair really good, so they can open some braid shops. But we won't discriminate, we'll give African Americans loans, we'll just find a way to make their interest rates a little higher, so if their business is not successful, we can force them closed a little quicker.

Next, we will come up with a plan on how to give less money and funds to city schools. Make the school lunch programs less nutritious. We will shut down and close all the school programs that help kids with their curriculums. Shut down all recreation centers. Shut down all summer camps; the kids can just hang out in their neighborhoods over the summer. Next on the agenda is finding ways to make it easier to get public assistance. Welfare, food stamps, and Section 8 housing; give it all to them, they deserve it. Let's come up with a plan to take fathers out of the household. Now this one could be hard, because there are some strong-minded men out there. But once we start with a few, this cycle can go on for generations to come.

One of the secret societies' members asked, "What if these vicious methods affect our good wholesome communities?" Well we will hide it like it doesn't exist. We will give treatments to help like psychiatrists, doctors, lawyers, and family support. Our goal here gentlemen, is an attempt to destroy a certain group of people. To make them poor, lazy, and dependent on the government. Make them delusional on what's going on around them. Make them think that the world consists of just their neighborhood. Make them feel as if drugs and liquor are the only way to feel good about yourself. So, let's close this meeting for today and come back and see if any of these things work.

After about five years in, I started to see things I probably would have never thought about if I wasn't a CO. First, about 30 to 40% of these guys come back after being released. The longer I've worked here (and anything after five years is considered a veteran), I've notice the same guys come back and forth. To some, it is like a revolving door (sad but true). Was the secret society thing working (lol)? I started to hear the same stories. "Yeah I just got caught with a little weed". Or "I just got a parole violation".

A parole violation can consist of not giving your parole agent your address or new telephone number, failing to go see them, failing a urinalysis test, and the worst violation is committing another crime while you are already on parole. Or this one, "My baby mother said I hit her." I ask, "Well did you?" "Naw, CO. She had some Nigga in my house while I was locked up, so we started arguing and she called the police on me. I never laid a finger on her, but she told the police I was on parole. And they locked me up. Damn Bitch, I'm going to kill her when I get out." My response was, "So you mean to tell me, you want to change your parole sentence, which is probably less than a year, to a life sentence for murdering your baby's mother, in which you'll get 30 years plus. OoooooK. (Maybe the secret society meeting is working).

Being I got 5+ years working in the jail, the duty Lieutenants started assigning me to work different parts of the institution. Places like the medical unit, (I call it chest pain central). Inmates come to the medical unit, (most faking chest pains) to socialize with other inmates coming from other housing units in the jail. Or, to get their free medication provided by the State of Maryland. From time to time, we will have a fight in the jail and the injured inmates have to be assessed for their injuries, from the medical staff. I have seen injuries from busted lips, black eyes, or some serious stab wounds. The medical staff will patch them up and either send them back to their housing unit, or the injuries are real serious, enough to send them out to one of the local hospitals.

Not the greatest place to work, but for me it was a change of pace from working in housing units for the past five years. I also started to get the duties of escort and relief. The relief officers would relieve the other officers on their posts for their lunch breaks. We also were their first responders, if there were any emergencies in the institution - like fights, fires, and medical emergencies. If the inmate was fighting, we would escort him first to medical unit to get assessed and then escort him to the segregation unit. (Jail within Jail). And speaking of the Segregation Unit, they started assigning me there, as well. Even though the inmates were locked down at least 23 hours a day, these guys may be the worst, most disrespectful, and craziest (mentally ill) inmates you can have in your institution.

I remember one day, I was making my rounds in the segregation unit and I looked into a cell and there was an inmate laying under his bunk. I knocked on the door and ask, "Are you okay"? He said, "Get the Fuck away from my door." He then came out from under his bunk. He started patting the middle of his arm. He then took out a pretend needle and filled it with his pretend drugs. Watching, and saying to myself "Unbelievable," he took the pretend needle and I guess shot the pretend drugs in the veins of his arm. He then closed his eyes and said, "That's some good shit. Fuck, I'm high as shit." He opened his eyes, looked at me watching him, amazed, and said, "Hey CO. you want some of this dope?" I said, "Naw, I'm good, you go ahead and enjoy the rest of that."

I guess he did, because once I came back to his cell, after doing my rounds he was laying under his bunk, giggling and laughing. Another of many incidents that I remember. Once again making my rounds. An inmate knocked on his door and said, "CO, can I get some toilet paper?" I kindly said, "We're all out, but I'll find some and get it to you shortly." Oh, my goodness he goes off. "Fuck you, you bitch ass nigga, When I Get Uptown, I'm going to kill your ass and your family!" I'm thinking to myself, *over some toilet paper.* (lol). But it was a threat to my life and my family, so I had to write this up.

When an inmate breaks any rules of the institution. (Fights, threats, destruction of state property, etc.), any staff can write up an infraction on an inmate, describing what rule he has broken and how he will be charged. The inmate was served with his infraction write up. He signed and acknowledged it. The next day while making my rounds, the same segregation unit, the same inmate says "A Yo I knew you was going to write me up, but I don't give a fuck, segregation is jail within Jail." My response to that may not have been professional, but I had to get my point across. "Listen, I didn't write you up to keep you on segregation, I wrote you for my protection and to cover me. What you inmates, I guess are too stupid to realize is, that we CO's grew up and were raised in the same streets you inmates were raised in. We just made better decisions in our lives to do better.

Since then, working here and getting firearms qualified and having a military background made it easy for me to acquire a gun permit to carry a weapon with me, and yes, I do carry. So, if I ever see you on the streets, without hesitation, I'm shooting you first. If I have to go to court for murder or attempted murder, my defense is going to be this copy of this write up that you signed, stating how you were going to kill me and my family if you saw me uptown. Your Honor, I feared for my life and he came at me in an aggressive way. So, I'll give you something to think about, because you're not going nowhere, no time soon. So, think about I got a permit to carry and paperwork that's signed by you, stating how you are going to kill me. if you saw me. And remember a dead man can't testify. And I walked away. What have I become. They say the longer you're in corrections, it changes you. The conditions and the atmosphere, take a toll on you physically and mentally. Whatever religion you believe in, it is mandatory to have a good prayer before and after work.

Another spot or unit in the jail I started to get assigned to a lot was 3B. This housing unit was assigned to the working men or trustees we had working in various parts of the institution like Dietary, the Storeroom, Maintenance, Sanitation, Receiving, and we also had outside workers who would go out to dump trash and clean around the institution. They also did things like shovel snow in the winter. The inmates in this housing unit were coming and going all day long. To the unit, back-and-forth to work, so you really had to keep track of where everyone was, especially during count time. The showers were open longer, and the recreation is pretty much all day.

We shut everything down at count times, and at the end of the 3 to 11 shift. They have small TVs and radios in their cells. Since they get paid for their labor of the work they do throughout the institution, they accumulate more commissary than regular inmates, who hope their loved ones send them money to buy snacks and hygiene products. I tell you these inmates think they have it so good that they forget they are still in jail. Sometimes they test policies and procedures of the jail, only because of their workingmen status. They think they can break certain rules and get away with it. I admit, some officers play the Super Cop role and don't allow them to get away with nothing, which can bring attention to the unit.

Some officers have closed their eyes to everything and just let these workingmen or trustees run amuck. That leads to a loud and sometimes uncontrollable housing unit. Then there are officers like myself. I would say I'm in between. I understand that you're an inmate trustee, and you have a little bit more privileges then a regular inmate. But you're still an inmate. So, respect me and the rules of the institution, and I'll respect you. I'm not that super cop that yells, "Hold the Fucking noise down," during recreation. But I'll try to be professional, walk up to a group of guys that are loud and say, "Gentlemen, please keep the noise down, I can't hear myself think." They'll laugh, and I get the "okay Officer Bryant, you got that."

As grown men, I give you respect; I think you should give it back. A lot of the trustees/workingmen, you get to know pretty well, because they're doing their incarceration time here at MRDCC. Most of the guys have less than three years; so, seeing those in the unit, or whether they work the institution, you get to know them pretty well. Having brief conversations with them seemed interesting. The conversations were usually not about their crime, because I didn't care about that and didn't want to judge anyone. But, it usually was about seeing them where they worked, and how they can use those same skills when they get out there on the streets. *Yes, COs were social workers* (lol). I asked guys who worked as electricians, plumbers, dietary workers, and sanitation workers.

Several conversations went similar to this. To me, the work that you are doing now, is the same work you could've been doing out of jail. Most inmates would say, "I know, I was being lazy selling drugs; it was easy and generated fast money (secret society meeting). Most inmates would say that, by being here, I've learned what I'd have done wrong and will try to do better when I get out. Bryant is working hard, making minimum wage at McDonald's, and trying to support yourself and your family. So, I ask out of curiosity, "What do you make here as a working man?" Most reply, "Well it depends on where you work, but it averages from .30-.90 cents an hour." Of course, I had a surprised look on my face and said, "I'm not here to judge, but you complain about minimum wage with your freedom, work for less than a dollar an hour, and are locked up. Right now, I'm not even going to try to figure that one out."

They usually reply, "I know, Officer Bryant." He said some dudes that are locked up will get out and do the right thing; then there are some that get out and do the same dumb shit that got them here. Me, playing my CO/ Counselor role, I tell most guys, "You must have a plan." There's a saying I heard that goes," he who does not plan, plans to fail. Its little conversations like that, that sometimes make me wonder, *was this my calling to work in corrections?* Maybe God put me here to help steer some lost sheep on the right path. To try to put some sense in some minds that were corrupt by the so-called system.

One thing I do know is that I am truly blessed. No, I'm nowhere near perfect; but talking to some of these guys, I'm glad that I am in front of The Bars and not behind them. Because then there are some conversations between inmate to inmate, like the one I heard in the segregation unit that made me shake my head. Let me paint the picture.

First, there's an inmate on the top tier talking to an inmate on the bottom tier. Inmate on the top tier name is A-YO (I#1). Inmate on the bottom tier is named Black (I#2). Second, if you see the word right, looking like *riiight,* pronounce and add those extra syllables so you can get a better jest of the conversation. Here we go. (I#1) A Black! (I#2) What up Yo. (I#1) I say right! (I#2) Riiight. (I#1) Who's working today? (I#2) Officer Bryant, and I don't know the other officer. (I#1) Oh, I say right! (I#2) Riiight. (I#1) I'am up here laying in the cut, right. (I#2) Riiight. (I#1) And I was thinking right. (I#2) Riiight. (I#1) What I was going to do, once I get uptown. (I#2)

Riiight. (I#1) I'm sell one of my BMWs, right. (I#2) Riiight. (I#1) Go buy a couple of Keys (cocaine) right. (I#2) Riiight. (I#1) Set up shop right. (I#2) Riiight. (I#1) Flip them keys right. (I#2) Riiight. (I#1) And do me. (I#1) I'm kept the stash over one of my bitches' house right. (I#2) Riiight. (I#1) Break her off a little something right. (I#2) Riiight. (I#1) And come up. (I#1) A-YO I say right! (I#2) Riiight. (I#1) You feel me? (I#2) Riiight. (I#1) I say right. (I#2) Riiight. (I#1) Shit going be lovely! (I#1) I say right. (I#2) Riiight. (I#1) Gear going be tight. (That means his clothes going to be nice) (lol) Now you try to be deaf ears to these so-called conversations.

But working in the segregation unit is kind of boring, because there is not much going on. So, these types of conversations are entertaining, yet scary, at the same time. As a society and community, where have we failed? Lack of parenting, schooling, and role models. There were hundreds of leaders and role models who sacrificed their time and effort to keep our communities and neighborhoods from looking the way they look today. Will the chain ever be broken?

Being I was weapons qualified, I also got assigned from time to time to work outside hospital details. Inmates sometimes will get hurt or injured from fighting, or really get sick (real chest pains). They would be hospitalized at one of the local hospitals for a brief period of time. (Free hospital stay, courtesy of State Taxpayers) The offices are equipped with all the restraints to keep the inmate restrained to the bed. And of course, we carry weapons. Hospital duties wasn't a bad jig. You just have to be on your job making sure the inmate wasn't trying to escape, because we were outside the institution. The hospital room became the cell, and we had to make sure the inmate didn't harm herself or hospital staff that came in the room to treat him.

The inmate cannot receive any visitation from his family or friends while in the hospital, unless he was about to die from his illnesses, in which all visitations had to be approved by the warden of the institution. After good days/bad days in the institution, to get placed on a hospital detail was great to me because it got you out of the routine foolishness of the jail. You just hope you have an alert and good Officers working with you. I'm not going to sit here and lie on myself, there may have been a few times where I may have drifted off, but I pop right back up because I realize we're at work, sitting with an inmate who may have a bright idea to try to escape. But you don't want to be working with someone that they're in such a deep sleep to where their snoring.

The supervisors, from time to time, come out to check on you during the shift. And the last thing they want to do is catch both officers asleep with the inmate cuffed to the bed. Not a good look. That could be prime time for an inmate to plan his escape. I sometimes would think how the officers would feel if they fell asleep, woke up and the inmate was gone. You could kiss that nice State job goodbye. Cancel Christmas!

CHAPTER FIVE

WHERE THE MEN AT?

2000 zero zero party over with, out a time. So tonight, I'm going to party like its 1999. (A line from a great musical artist Prince) But yes, we are in the new millennial, the 2000's. As far as all the party and joy of my job is gone. Some days I just feel so disgruntled. The inmates have seemed to wear me down, and mainly for the fact that all these grown-ass men fall short of the American dream and think it's all about crime. My tolerance for stupidity is gone (lol). But I refuse to be a statistic, so I get my butt out of bed and push it on into work.

Hold that thought for a moment about how corruptions, I mean corrections, is wearing me out. I would like to take a moment to talk about my other life and why I drag myself into work. Okay, let's not forget that I was single and always ready to mingle. But most men, not all, there comes a time when a single life is for the birds, and you just want to settle down. My friend Brian introduced me to RK (I'm not going to put her government name out there). Now, I thought this was going to be a long-lasting relationship; but things didn't happen that way and I guess the chemistry wasn't really there, yet, we still remain friends.

A great part of the relationship that should be a joy to any man, (but not all) is that we had a son. Yup, my baby boy Aaron. But like I said the relationship turned into a friendship, and once again, I was single and ready to mingle. The dating scene is cool, but being raised in a two-parent household, by my stepdad and mom, marriage life is what I really wanted. But I started dating women who really didn't know what they wanted. I know I don't have the looks of the supermodel, the body of an athlete, or making a six-figure income. But I have been told that I'm a nice-looking man. When time presents itself, I am in the gym, and I do make a decent income with benefits (lol). Ladies listen, I'm not an expert on love and relationships. But I'll share what I have: experience listening to friends, coworkers, and my own life experience.

Fifty percent of all men date, and eventually get married when they think they found the right one. I call it the five-year rule. If you date a man over five years, and he has not proposed, you're not the one. I'm sure a lot of people disagree, and that's fine because, like I said, I'm not an expert. But challenge him, and propose to him, and see what he says. The bottom line is, don't waste your time.

The next Twenty-Five percent of men (and I am breaking the guy code by leaking this info) are players for life. Never, never, never, ever, have they any intentions of getting married. They would be in a relationship with you over 10 years (wasting your time) but marriage is out of the question.

Then the last Twenty-Five percent of what I hear females saying all the time, is: "They are either gay or locked up!" Now the Gay part I can't speak on. But, I can contest to the lockup part, most definitely. There are so many men (non-eligible bachelors) that are locked up, it's ridiculous. They can be out here being productive citizens, but they chose to be incarcerated. Anyway, I'm the part of that Fifty percent who want to find the woman of my life and get married. I believe some people are put into your life for a reason. I was reignited with a woman who I didn't know personally but knew of. Her name is Janice.

She and I started to date, and making a love story short, after about two years we got married. She already had two kids, a son (Damion) and a daughter (Brittany), which didn't bother me because I loved her and raised them like they were my own; and as you already know, I had a son. And together, we share two amazing daughters (Jazmine and Lauren). Through God's blessing, I'm living the American dream. But folks, let me tell you, marriage is tricky. I learned that definitely you're not going to agree on everything. Sometimes, there will be arguments over the dumbest stuff. And having a stressful job like corrections, my blood pressure was through the roof. But, if you truly love your partner, you realize that the good times outweigh the bad times; and you strive to make the marriage work and be successful.

Being married with children gives me the strength to push forward and be the man of the household that supports his family. My family needs me, so I dragged myself in that belly of the beast institution to make sure my family is supported. I was raised in a two-parent household, but my dad was not my biological father. Being such, I've learned that no matter what, all the kids you raise in your household, whether they're yours, step-kids, or a family member's child that you have now, who has come to come live with you. Show them love. Do your best to mold their futures so that they are successful. Teach them to love and not hate themselves, or other people. Never knowing my biological father made me, I admit, a little disgruntled; but at the same time, made me positive in my thinking that if I ever had kids, I would do my best to be a part of their lives.

I'll share a quick, and I do mean quick story of mine. I was about 30 years old and I got a call from one of my aunts that my biological father would like to meet me. Seriously, is this a late April fool's joke. It wasn't, so I entertain the notion of meeting. She gave me his telephone number and said, "He's looking forward to hearing from you." I know you're reading this book, but just imagine the surprised look on my face when I was told that. After 30 years, I'm sure you are looking forward to hearing from me, but I should've been hearing from you a long time ago. But, I called this stranger, and we talked for about five minutes, if that. Reluctantly, I agreed to come to his house to meet with him.

So, my wife, two daughters, and I travel to the west side of Baltimore City to meet him. (Lafayette Avenue for any Baltimoreans out there) I got there at the time we chose to meet, of course he wasn't there:

typical. This little boy, probably around 10 to 12 years old, sat on the stairs in front of the house. I asked him if he knew the guy who lived there; and he said he wasn't home yet. I said okay, let him know I came by. Just when I was about to leave, a car pulled up and there he was; well I think it was him because remember I had never seen the man. But it was him. He introduced himself and so did I, trying to be cordial. Then he said to the little boy, do you know who this is. The little boy had a surprised look on his face and as if I can read his mind he would say, "hell no, who is this"? He said that's your older brother. Wow awkward, for me and the little boy.

Again, I'm in my 30s and this little boy is about 12, not a very welcoming moment. Anyway, we talked for about another 10 to 15 minutes, and he suggested on reuniting over the summer for a cookout, or something that he was going to have over his house, and how he wanted me and my family to attend. After that short conversation was over, I left. The man who waited over 30 years to try to seek me out, to me is unbelievable. Maybe I'm heartless for not feeling pressed, or at all concerned to see this guy again. My wife and maybe even some others may say so. But to me, where were you at, when I graduated from all the public schools? Where were you at, when I needed to learn how to drive? Where were you at when I needed guidance to stay out of trouble in growing up in the streets of Baltimore city, and making sound decisions to grow into a responsible man?

Yes, I thank God I had a stepdad, but we didn't have that close of a relationship to teach me all those things. I just kind of studied what he did as being a hard worker and a family man, who took responsibility for the people living in his household. Society sometimes would have you believe that if a father is not in his kid's life, generates a worthless boy to a worthless man. Not 100% true. Now don't get me wrong, working in the prison system, there are some men that their first excuse of them doing time is because they didn't have the father or role model in their life to teach them how to become a man.

Okay I sympathize a little (just a little). But when you're in your 30s, 40s, 50s or even your 60s doing the same dumb stuff and making the same mistake you did when you were a teenager or when you were in your early 20s…that's when I don't have much sympathy for you. You're a grown man, so grow up. Especially if you have children, raise them to be smart and not make the same mistakes you did. It's sometimes sad to see wives, girlfriends, and baby mothers bring the kids to visit their fathers on visiting days.

One of the things that's heartbreaking and sad, when a little girl breaks down and starts crying when the visit is over. Yelping "Daddy, I don't want you to go back in there!" Daddy, I love you and miss you when you coming home? Boo-Hoo Boo-Hoo." Even some of the little boys start crying when the visit is over. But I have seen little boys already wearing gang colors and paraphernalia to show their father they have love for those streets. But the only love that should be focused on is those little girls and boys you left crying in the visiting room. The love should be your motivation to get out and stay out.

Once again, I don't judge what got you here. But I do say to some, do the right thing and stay out, and if anything, show your children the love that they need, so they won't come in here.

The 2000's brought changes to the world. YouTube and Facebook were launched. A devastating disaster happened in New Orleans with Katrina. And a bill was passed. A call for "No Child Left Behind". My point on that is it created a percentage of kids in public school to pass on a low curriculum of standards, needed to get to the next grade. Yes, it helps kids pass to the next grade and even graduate from high school. But was your skill level able for you to compete in the world of college or filling out a job application correctly for employment. No child left behind got you a diploma, but can you read or write to put together an effective resume for a career? The great singer/musician, Marvin Gaye, was before his time; but I always think about his song, *What's Going On?* Years ago, a crime bill was passed to help keep petty crime criminals off the streets. And it did! (lol)

Working in law enforcement as a correctional officer, I witness a high-volume of men and women filling up the jails at an astonishing rate. Housing units were getting filled up by parole violators, and men with small crimes. Let me make myself clear: drugs are illegal, but if you get arrested for having drug paraphernalia on you, like a crack pipe with a little residue in it and you get years in jail, something is slightly wrong with this system. And as a correctional facility, we are feeling the effects of this so-called crime bill.

Now I know it takes much more than me saying this. But the most effective way to cut crime and save States, not thousands, but billions of dollars in the future, is to spend less taxpayers' dollars in the police force, more taxpayers' dollars in education. More money, books, and computers. More money and afterschool programs, and tutoring. More money in gymnasiums and recreational/athletic leagues. Your money and school lunch programs, making them more nutritious for the kids.

Now here's a big one. Give the teachers that teach and mold our kids' higher salaries. The salaries between a state police and a teacher are almost double. Now, be honest. Whose career has a greater impact in each community - a teacher or the police? If most of the things I just mentioned, happen in the United States Inner Cities (where if you check the facts, crime rates are higher). This is what I think - simple changes would drop crime rate dramatically and slowly, but surely, in the future, send less people to jail and make more people productive citizens. Excuse me for just venting for a moment. He He He, back to corrections.

Making my rounds, one day in the house housing unit, an inmate asked me; 'Hey CO what time is it?" Me, (in my "Why the hell are you asking me what time it is" voice) "Why do you want to know the time, you got to go to work?" Ha Haaa, I snickered. The inmate said,

"No I gotta Fucking Pray!" I said to him, "How you going to use Fucking and Pray in the same sentence?" I just shook my head and walked away. Disrespecting whom he prays to like that.

With nine years plus in, these are the little things that take my stress-level through the roof. This job will do that to you. You may come to work, feeling great and friendly, great that your coworkers are there with a pleasant attitude; but by the end of the day, this job sometimes (not all the time) but sometimes, wants to make you stop at your local liquor store and get something strong to drink (lol). Well, like I said. I got a little over nine years and I need a change. Not out of corrections, but a different scenery in this facility. So, I put in for a shift change.

There's a saying that goes, "you can change the frame of a photo, but the picture remains the same." I needed a different look. I'll change the frame, but corrections will remain the same. Ironically, about two weeks later, my Shift Captain called me, while I was on my post. He said "Officer Bryant, the Transportation Unit needs a couple of officers to work in their unit, would you be interested in going. I said, "The transportation unit, OK, can you give me a couple of days to think about it?" (That way I can get more time to ask around and find out what they do.) He, sounding a little arrogant said, "No, you can't wait a couple of days; I need to know now".

Well Damn! (That's not what I said, but I thought it.) I thought for a second. *Well, to be on Transportation, I will be working daylight hours, instead of working this 3 to 11 shift. I'll get out the jail every day because transportation transports the inmates to court and other State Correctional Institutions in MD. And the best thing about Transportation is that they have weekends and holidays off. This is the frame I needed to change.* And I said, "Yes I'll take it. One week later my adventure of working in the Transportation Unit began.

Working in transportation gave me a bigger perspective of the judicial system. It starts with a person committing a crime on the streets. They are arrested and taken to a local county or city jail. If sentenced by a Judge or Jury, they are sent to a State Correctional Center, like the one I presently work at. And once they are classified, they are then sent to a State Prison where they would do their sentenced time. That's where the transportation unit comes into play. We give them a thorough search, put restraints on them, and carry them to their State Institution. (A good piece of advice for inmates, especially the ones at these large institutions, is that when you take a shower, don't drop the soap, because a lot of men are going to be looking at your booty) (lol) In Maryland, we have State Prisons in Baltimore city, and in the counties of Jessup, Eastern Shore, Hagerstown and Cumberland.

My seeing it firsthand, just amazes me about the number of guys we transport to these facilities on a daily basis. For some, not all, reality really starts to set in when you're in restraints on this bus, heading to a correctional facility. The only time you are really going to see your loved ones now, is if they have time to visit you on a visiting day.

Most of my tour of duty on the Transportation Unit, I was on the court detail. Monday through Friday, I would take inmates to court. I've seen the most hard-core criminals become very humble when they stood in front of a judge, trying to get their sentence reduced. (No, your Honor, yes, your honor) A lot of judges I feel were fair at a sentencing (who am I to judge); but it is hard to reduce your sentence when you have to face the same judge three or four times. Judges be saying things like, "so Mr. you're in my court again?" The inmate would say, "well you honor what had happened was…"

The Judge would cut them off and say, "No need to explain, this is the fourth time you've been at my courtroom and I told you if you ever faced me again, that I will give you the maximum penalty allowed." Hell, what can the Inmate say? It's time to face the consequences. Working in transportation and taking these guys to court, I never wanted to know these guys' crime, but hearing about what these guys crimes were, made me sympathetic of the inmate population. It is said that African-American males get tougher sentencing. In some cases, maybe.

Because I have seen the same crime committed by two different races, but different sentencing was handed out. But don't get me wrong, I have seen all races, colors, and religions, get sentenced by the court of law. And the law of the land is the law of the land; if you do the crime, you will get the time. Transportation unit was interesting to work at, to say the least. When inmates go from and back to their institutions, they must be strip searched. They take off all their clothing. We search the clothing for contraband, such as: weapons, cell phones, cigarettes and drugs. We have them raise their hands to check under their arm pits, then lift their genital areas, and then turn around to squat and cough.

You'd be amazed of the stuff guys try to stick in their rectum to try to hide. We, as officers, try to conduct this search with the utmost respect and professionalism. But we always get feedback from the inmates with comments like," you just want to see my dick," or "C O trying to look up my ass, he must be gay." Not at all, sir; we do this to stop contraband from leaving and coming into the facility. Okay now, get this. I love to share this story. Sometimes, while working the transportation unit, you'd get assigned the transportation bus. We would transport inmates to Hagerstown, Maryland, the home of three large Maryland state correctional institutions.

Now let me paint the picture. Most of the institutions in the Baltimore and Jessup region were employed by a majority of African-American Officers. Hagerstown, Eastern Shore, and Cumberland were employed by a majority of white Officers. For some strange reason, the inmates disrespected us more in the Baltimore and Jessup region. But, when they got up to the Hagerstown Mountains, (they say home of the Good Ole Boys) they were a bit more respectful to those officers. I'm not making this up.

Anyway, we did our routine strip search and got all kinds of negative feedback. But when we got on the bus, this want-to-be gang member inmate demeanor changed. The funny thing is, when we got them there, we stood by, while they conducted their strip search. Now, I witnessed this myself. Their strip search went as follows. Take off all your clothes. Put them in that bag. Lift your hands up. Take your hands, run them through your hair. Take your hands, lift up your penis and nut sacs. Turn around, lift your feet one at a time. Now get this. Take your hands, spread your butt cheeks, squat then cough. Turn around, take your hands to open up your mouth and stick your tongue out. And then get dressed. Holdup! Did anybody catch that? The last thing they did, was take their hands, open up their butt cheeks, then take their same hands after being in their butt and open up their mouth.

Ironically the inmates did not have any problems and any negative feedback to these officers' search. Let me say this again, we get called all kinds of bitches, faggots, and cursed out daily for proper search. But when you had your hand in your ass, then in your mouth, you say nothing. Unbelievable. That's that BS. When we had to transport inmates back to Baltimore from Hagerstown. Once we get these guys on the bus, the bus is quiet. The ride was about 45 minutes. Once you hit the Baltimore County lines, the noise and talking begins. It was like zombies that had just woken up out of their trance.

I guess the city air got life back in them, or something. Once again, being on transportation unit gave me a little freedom to get out of the jail and learn and see different things of the corrections.

After working on the Transportation Unit for about a year and a half, the 7 to 3 shift was taking requests to transfer on that shift, so I put my request in. I'd figured, I went back to work inside the jail, I would prefer to be on dayshift instead of the evening shift. A couple of weeks later, my request was granted, 7 to 3 shift here I come. Let's see what this shift has in store for me.

In the mid-2000's Maryland Corrections, mainly in the Baltimore region, was changing. That was not a lot of people applying for the job, especially males. So, someone, way over my pay grade decided two things. One, let's lower the Hiring Age to 18 instead of 21. Now that's cool if you were 18 years old. You get a nice career making about 33,000 thousand dollars a year; and with overtime you can make well over 50 to $60,000 range. Not bad for an 18 or 19-year-old graduating from high school. The bad news for corrections, is they hope that these younglings were mentally stable enough to deal with these inmates.

Making a long story short, these younglings were easy targets for the inmates, who were Masters of manipulation. As for inmates, most who really don't want to follow institutional rules anyway, it's even harder for a grown man to accept an 18 or 19-year-old, telling them what to do. This hiring practice didn't last too long. And correctional officials found out quickly that this was a mistake. Now don't get me wrong, there were some younglings that made it. They were even mature enough to handle the life of a correctional officer. But some fell at the wayside. A few were manipulated by the inmates and population, and they were either fired or quit, months after being hired.

The second hiring practice, people way above my pay grade did, (I hate to go here but this is a true story lol) was take women off welfare and public assistance and give them a State job. (Like in the Maryland State of Corrections) Yup, I said it. Stop living off the state and start working for it. Not a bad idea. But here's the positives and negatives. Yes, we started getting more officers hired. Once again, coming in making about $33,000 a year. And if you had a good babysitter, or someone you felt comfortable with watching your kids, you can make a lot of overtime, bumping your salary up to 40, 50, even $60 thousand a year.

Not bad. Much better than them, as they say, living off the state. The negative in all of this, in about two to three years, the officers in the Baltimore region were majority women. I will go to Roll Call; with about 45 officers at least 30 were women. That leaves about 15 males on a shift working in an all-male prison. Where are the Men At! Females got paid the same as males, but working in an all-male prison, there was a lot they couldn't do. Like strip search an inmate. For whatever reason, if the inmate needed to be strip searched, you would have to go find a male officer. If a housing unit called on the radio, a code for a fight or an unruly inmate, yes, all available staff would rush to the problem, but when you got on the elevator to go to the floor and you looked around and see 2 males and 10 females, this is a problem.

Now don't get me wrong, some of the female officers roll with the best of them. There were even some times, that you would rather have some of the females go to an incident, instead of some of the males. But with a 300-pound, musclebound, unruly inmate, you would like to have a little muscle there. I'm just saying. I hate to admit it, but sometimes it's true, that when male officers arrived on the scene of unruly inmates, there in fight mode, compared to some female officers, looking nice and smelling good to an inmate, who's been locked up for a couple of months or years, the presence of that female officer makes him calm down really quick.

Let's think about this for a second. They're locked up, with no companionship. (Well, then that all depends on how close he and his cellmate are, but I'm not going to go there) (lol) So you have all this testosterone buildup. And here comes this female officer. When inmates get around female officers, their whole demeanor changed. You would think they have a chance in hell of taking her out tonight. One thing I'm sure of is that being he hasn't been around females in a while, she will be on his mind tonight, as he lay in his cell. Now that's not what female officers were hired for, they have the same duties as anyone else. But working in an all-male institution, from time to time, being a female, worked to escalate some problems.

But if there was an inmate, ready to go to battle with any officer who came in their cell, we had to go in and get him out that cell. The search was on to get at least five male officers to put on riot gear and go into the cell to extract the inmate out. Most of the time, the supervisors would have to send female officers to certain posts to relieve male officers off their posts, just so they can have the five males they needed to put on riot gear and extract the inmate out of the cell.

I say again, "what happened to all the males?" Some say that they just couldn't pass the tests to become a correctional officer. Some may think they couldn't pass the drug or urinalysis tests. Some may say that there's just too many males locked up from the Baltimore city area. Are these stereotypes, and if so are the stereotypes fact or fiction? Nevertheless, there just weren't enough males in corrections at the time. My institution, the Maryland Reception Diagnostic and Classification Center and Baltimore City Detention Center, felt it was worse because these two institutions in the Baltimore region had transportation units, at which you definitely had to keep a higher percentage of male officers. Mainly, because of the strip search, that routinely has to be done leaving and coming back to the institutions. I can honestly say males were getting burnt out, due to the fact of the things that we were allowed to do, and females couldn't. Signs of the time.

To retire as a Maryland Correctional Officer, you need to do at least 20 years. Wow, I now have 11 years in, and I always look to try different things in corrections to help me break up the monotony and not succumb to the stress levels of having this job. Over the past 11 years, I have seen officers come and go. Keeping it real, some officers I knew are now borderline alcoholics. This job, if you let it, can affect you so much, that you want to take a drink before coming into work, or have a bottle in the car waiting for you, to get off your shift.

I know some officers, male and female who got off work and went home and took their frustrations out on their spouse or their kids. It's really sad when you come to work as an officer, but State Police comes to your job with a warrant for your arrest, because you stressed out and felt the need to smack your wife around, when you got home. You can forget securing this job after you have a charge of spousal abuse. Though we had random drug tests, there were not many, but a few officers pushed the envelope and took a chance of Baltimore City's choices of drugs, crack, heroin, and methadone.

I'm not one to judge, but why take the chance and mess up this good state job. So, I only drink on occasions, I don't do drugs, and I was raised to respect women as if they were my mom or my sister, so I'm definitely not going home and fighting my spouse. The way I cope with this job is to not become complacent, I try to switch it up with different duties of the job. I applied to take the Sgt. Test. I figured if I move up the ranks being a Sergeant would present new opportunities to do different things. And doing different things helps me not to become that violent drunk. So, I take the Sergeant test, and in a couple of weeks my test results came back.

My score was good enough to go through the next phase of getting promoted, and that was the Sgt. Interview. The Sergeant's Interview consists of sitting in front of a panel of three people; more than likely they are Lieutenants and Captains who ask you questions pertaining to the job, and how you would have conduct yourself in certain emergencies or situations that occur. I, for the most part, think I did fairly well for my first time taking this interview. But about a week later, a couple of officers got promoted, and I was at one of them.

Now like I said this was my first time taking it, so I really didn't feel bad for not getting it. But not to sound feminist, the thing that really was obvious is the ones who got promoted were females, who got only 4 to 5 years in, and I'm here sitting on almost 12 years. I know I'm not crazy because there were other male officers who felt the same way that I did. So, the rumors started spreading. Certain females that got promoted were dating or sleeping with certain lieutenants or captains. Made me wonder if getting promoted here is based on experience, tests or, an interview; or is it based on giving me what I want, and I will give you what you want. I am glad I didn't smoke weed, because I would be high as a kite trying to figure this one out. Oh well, maybe next year.

A tragic thing happened this year, when the levees in Louisiana broke. It was a horrible ordeal for many African-Americans living in that area. A Famous Rapper got on national TV and said the President doesn't care about black people. Fact or Fiction. All I know is that it's 2005 and we are still experiencing things like this. Now, in Baltimore city, we may not have levees break; but African Americans are killing each other at an alarming rate, and the numbers go up each year. And let's not even mention the drugs that are plaguing Baltimore city, like heroin and methadone.

Walking around the world-famous Lexington Market in downtown Baltimore city, where you can go and get any type of food you want to eat. This place looks like a scene from a Zombie movie. Drug addicts are nodding in a deep five-second sleep, then they're leaned over, but they never fall. Michael Jackson could have used them in his *Remember the Time* video, with the leans, and the *Thriller* video with the Zombie dance. If you're from Baltimore, you're kind of used to the scene, but as a Tourist visiting the city you're like, "What the hell?"

The good food with a different variety and vendors draw people to Lexington Market. Some mornings on my way to work, I stopped there to get a breakfast sandwich, (bacon and eggs and cheese on toast with jelly, of course) and the drug addicts are already in full effect. I notice it had to be an inflation for the drug-users on the scene. They used to ask you for spare change. Now it's "brother you have a dollar?" Wow. And don't let them see you putting change in your pocket. They're coming right at you. For the most part, I have my uniform on and my mean face and say, "I don't have any change or time right now." *What's going on with the city? Was going on with this job?* Female officers are taking over.

I can't get promoted, and if I was taking any kind of prescription medication this job will proceed my daily dose. (Lol) What's a man to do? I say to myself. *Think Lewis think.* I Pray, and Pray, and Pray. And then it hit me. My prayers were answered. I know, I'll transfer. Transfer to another institution. Start fresh somewhere else. I'll carry my state time, plus the new scene would be great. So, I put in my request to transfer in to a Correctional Institution, right down the street from here. Baltimore City Booking and Intake Center aka BCBIC. It will be hard leaving the friends I have grown with for the past 12 years, a few I even started the academy with. One thing for sure, MDRCC family (all staff) stays consistent in trying to keep that bond to stay friends forever. But my tour here is over, it's time to go. But they always say, be careful what you pray for.

CHAPTER SIX

CENTRAL BOOKING

Baltimore City Booking and Intake Center (BCBIC). My new facility for the next seven years. I have 13 years in, striving for this 20-year retirement. So, let's see, where should I begin with BCBIC, because this place is a book within itself. (lol) Let's start with the beginning. Now, even though this institution still falls under Maryland State Correctional facility, this institution is considered pretrial, meaning that arrestees have not gotten their state time yet. These guys and girls were locked up on the streets of Baltimore City. They are brought here because they committed some kind of crime in the city. It could be anything from trespassing to murder. From loitering to selling drugs. If it happened in Baltimore City, you're coming here.

Breaking it down a little further, once locked up and brought here to BCBIC by Baltimore City Police or a Sheriff's Department, within the next 24 hours, you're going to either be released, (maybe because you had a little petty crime like urinating in public alley) or you're going to see a court commissioner for a bail hearing. Based on your charge, bails can be set from $1 dollar up to $1 million, and of course you can get a "no bail", meaning you're not going anywhere. No bails are for serious charges like rape and murder. Now, based on the amount of your bail, if it's not ridiculously high, your loved ones, or a bails bondsman, can pay the money and bail you out. Like I said, this is pretrial; so, just because you're home on bail, you still have to go to court, eventually, for the charges of the crime that you were locked up for. You're just free to sit at home until your court date comes up.

Now, here's where the drama comes in. Let's say your bail is high, (like in the thousands) most people can't afford that, heck they have rent to pay, let's say you have a no bail; you will sit here at BCBIC for about 60 to 90 days and then get transferred to the infamous Baltimore City Detention Center (BCDC) a.k.a. steel side which is also a pretrial institution. Once transferred to BCDC you will be sent there and try to survive until your court date comes up for the crime committed. Now, as crowded as Baltimore City court system is, that could be from six months to a year, if not longer.

I would like to send a shout out to all the officers who ever worked over at Baltimore City Detention Center. Some may say BCBIC is considered a Zoo, well if that's the case, BCDC is considered a Jungle. But much love goes to officers on what they have to endure on a daily basis. Anyway, back to where I work - BCBIC. Now, lucky for me the Lieutenant that was in charge of assigning officers' duties and shift, (new or transfers) was someone I knew from my old institution. She and I worked together in the transportation unit. She got a lieutenant's promotion and transferred here to BCBIC about a year ago, and was able to secure an office gig. I remember her saying,

"I'm happy for you and your transfer to pretrial, but it is not much better than where we came from".

We laughed, and I said, "probably so, but I only got seven years to do, so by the time I figure out things here and get accustomed to pretrial, my time here should go quick". Since she knows me, she said, "Usually I don't do this, placement here is on an as-needed basis". Since you're a 12-year veteran and I do know you, I'll keep you on dayshift, since that's where you were when you transferred from MRDCC. And out of the kindness of my heart, I'll give you an option. See said, "Central Booking (BCBIC) is broken up into two sections".

You can either go to the Receiving, Booking and Intake part of the building, or Security. The Lieut. gave me a breakdown between the two. Receiving, Booking, and Intake is on the first floor of the building. It is where police bring in the arrestees and they get booked, fingerprinted, ID, and then see a Court Commissioner. Based on their crime if their bail is too high they go to the Intake Unit to get searched. After that, they proceed to the second part of this institution, which is Security. These housing units on to third, fourth, and fifth floors and they stay here for 30 to 60 days until transferred to BCDC. Oh okay, so when I heard housing units as part of Security, it wasn't hard for me to choose the Receiving, Booking and Intake unit as my option to where I wanted to work. For some reason, without explaining she said, "Good choice".

Well Bryant, your official day to start is tomorrow; but today I'll give you a little tour of the building and later you have to go over to the Jail Industry building a.k.a. JI and get your new uniforms. Now, we wore the same State Correctional uniforms, only difference is the patches on the sleeve of our shirts say Maryland Division of Pretrial, and not Maryland Division of Corrections. I said, "Sounds good," and we were off on our tour. Central booking takes up almost a whole city block.

The floors of this building were long hallways that are divided up by three towers (north, center, and south) and on the third, fourth, and fifth floor were the security housing units that housed the arrestees waiting to go over to BCDC. Since I'm accustomed to working in housing units, this is where we went first. The layout was a little different from where I came from. The housing units on each floor had an officer working in a middle sally port area, which divided an Alpha and Bravo Unit. In the Alpha and Bravo Units, the inmate cells were on one level instead of two from where I came from.

Also, being that Central Booking was a newer facility, pretty much, the housing units were operated on an electronic system. Pushing buttons to open cell doors, hell at MRDCC we had to use those big old keys to open doors. Well after chit chatting with a few Officers about their duties working here, we moved on to another floor in a different tower. We arrived in the South towers. Basically, the same layout, difference is instead of cells, the inmates were set up in a dorm setting. Working in these housing units you definitely had to pay attention and be aware because these inmates were out all day 24/7.

They say some Officers prefer to work in a dorm setting and some don't. Me personally. I don't care because we all get the same pay no matter where you work. I think Officers who are subject to work in dorms should get an incentive or hazard pay from having to have these inmates in your face all day. Yes, it was a different scenery from MRDCC, but I guess after working 13 years in Corrections, nothing is different. "Ok," the lieutenant replied, "Let's go to the Receiving, Booking, and Intake area where you'll be working at."

This area took up pretty much the whole second floor. Now listen reader, (that's you) you must paint the picture as we toured the Receiving, Booking, and Intake areas. We walked through each area as if someone has gotten locked up in Baltimore City (home of The Wire). First, we went through the male sally port (there's a sally port for the females as well). The first thing that caught my eye or should I say would catch anybody's eye, was the two long benches filled with arrestees. All were sitting with their hands behind their backs, restrained with flex cuffs (that's plastic handcuffs). Each bench held about 6 to 7 guys. Now that's a site within itself, but that's not the half of it.

The officer working this post basic duties is to open the sally port door when Baltimore City Police arrive with people that were locked up in Baltimore City. The sally port, like I said, held about 13 arrestees, so if there were more than that in the sally port, the Police or Sheriff Departments would line their arrestees up outside the sally port door, until there was room on the bench for their arrestees to sit down. Now, you may ask, "Why are all these guys in the sally port waiting?" Okay I'll tell you. First, they have to get signed in by the officer working in the sally port. The officer gets the police that brings them in information and then gets the arrestees information.

Next there's a Nurse waiting to see the arrestees coming in the door. The nurse's job is to diagnose whether they're physically or mentally able to come into Central Booking. We're talking about people coming in straight off the streets, so it's a strong possibility that some may be drunk, high on drugs, or let's say physically injured by the police, (but that's a whole another story). If an arrestee is deemed physically unable to enter BCBIC the police or sheriff must take them to the hospital and get them cleared from a physician before they could come enter BCBIC. If an arrestee comes to the door yelling that he has injuries from the police department, the nurse immediately rejects them, and the police have to take them back out to a hospital.

Now the police don't like to hear that the arrestee is rejected from entering, but the State of Maryland Corrections will not be responsible for any arrestee's injuries that happened before they entered this building. Arrestees will get into holding cells waiting on the next process of being booked, he'd kick on the cell door and yell out saying "my ribs are broken" and being that the nurse accepted him makes it look like the correctional staff caused his injuries. We do not need those type of problems.

The second reason there are so many people in the sally port is because the police and sheriff departments really keep us busy; it's an amazing thing to see. The police vans would pull up, and sometimes two or three arrestees will get off the van; come back again and six to eight arrestees would get off the van. Unbelievable. I know it is not the police's fault, but if I didn't work here or see this for myself, I would never believe that so many people get locked up on a daily basis.

I'm not naïve to think that people don't get arrested every day, but the numbers that you see coming into Central booking is astonishing. So now you have about 13 guys in the sally port, but about 25 guys are lined up outside waiting to get in, it's a crazy sight to see. All these guys and gals who got locked up somewhere in Baltimore City are now lined up outside this sally port, waiting to get in and be processed.

The only time I see these kinds of lines are Black Friday, shoppers waiting to get into Walmart, voting lines with voters waiting to cast their vote, waiting in front of GameStop when the new NFL Madden game comes out for PlayStation and Xbox, or waiting for the tennis shoe store to open for the new Jordan's. And let me make this clear, as I say throughout this book, these are men and women of all races, all religions, and all ages. (I didn't want anyone to get the illusion that these are all young black males.)

The third reason the sally port benches are all filled up is the next post we visited, also the next process coming into BCBIC. And that is the Search Room. This is normally a two-officer post. One at a time, the officers have the arrestees come into the search room. The officers then cut off his flex cuffs and search their property, their clothes, and then the arrestee. We don't want any contraband coming into this state facility - weapons, drugs, cell phone, etc. Also, if the arrestee has any money it is counted and sealed in an envelope.

The next stop for us, or process for arrestees coming into Central booking is the actual Booking Window booth. The arrestees are handcuffed to these booths and booked in. This basically means officers working these stations get as much information from the arrestee as possible and put it into a database. And from what I understand once the arrestee is booked into the system, all their information is reviewed by a State's Attorney. The State's Attorney deems on whether they get release for what they were locked up for, or whether they go through a process to see a Court Commissioner. And the only way they'll get released for their charge or the crime they committed is to post a bail for their arrests, but they'll still eventually have to go to court for the charge they committed.

The next post we visited, or process for an arrestee, is to get photographed and fingerprinted. Oh boy, you've done it now. This is where the term Mug Shot comes from (lol). I guess the look on their faces for being locked up would generate an ugly mug. Of course, your fingerprints and photo go into a State and Federal criminal database. Also, the photo is used to make you an ID card, so we can identify you while you're in this fine facility. The next process for the arrestee is a waiting game.

The arrestees are put into bullpens or holding cells. The holding cells are in these long hallways of the booking floor. We called them A and B hallways. There are about 7 to 8 holding cells in each hallway. Each holding cell can hold comfortably about 10 to 12 arrestees. But walking down these hallways, at first glance, you see arrestees sitting on benches, laying on the floors or standing at the windows. It looks like a lot more than 15 to 20 arrestees in these holding cells. And every last one of these cells are filled to capacity. I think anyone seeing these packed holding cells filled with arrestees, for the first time, would say: "What the Hell...?" (I did).

Now the theory is, once you were booked at the booking window earlier, you have up until 24 hours see a Court Commissioner. I would like to say all the staff at BCBIC do a great job in making this process happen. Like the next post we visited, which is the Court Commissioner side that is in the A hallway. The officers working this post locate the arrestees out of one of these crowded holding cells (this sometimes can be challenging because of the number of arrestees) and put them in a Court Commissioner's both.

Here's where the Court Commissioners determine the arrestees fate. Based on your arrests, two things can happen while seeing the Court Commissioner - you're either getting a bail ($1 on up or a No Bail) or you'll be getting released. After the conference with the Court Commissioner, the officers could pretty much see the expression on the arrestee's face, wherever he got a bail, or was getting released. They are either frowning, crying, mad, happy, or smiling with joy. The officers take the arrestees out of the booth and either take them to the Release Area or put them in the cell that is called the Intake Cell. And that was our next stop on our tour - the Intake and Release Area.

The Release Area is a very critical area where only sergeants and lieutenants work. They release arrestees to go home, but as I said all I's must be dotted and all T's must be crossed, because the last thing they want to do is release an arrestee who wasn't supposed to be released. All paperwork must be checked and checked again.

Right next to the Release Area is the Intake Area. Officers working in this area's duties are to pull the inmates that were put into the Intake Holding Cell, (which is packed, of course) fully strip-search the arrestee; give them a BCBIC orange jumpsuit; give him his ID card, and basic essentials like sheets, towels, soap, etc. After all this is done, the officers escort him up to one of the security floors in one of the towers, where he will be sitting for 30 to 60 days. Then the arrestee will go over to BCDC where they'll wait until their court date comes up. Boom, and that's the whole process for an arrestee coming into BCBIC and the end of our tour through the Booking floor.

Being more than halfway to my 20-year retirement, with 13 to 14 years in, I still call this my halfway point. Mainly because this is a new institution for me, and I will be experiencing new things. And it didn't take long for me to be experiencing these new things. For the first couple of months to a year, I mainly worked in either the Search Room, or, back in Intake. And between the two on any given day, it's know telling what's going to happen.

In the Search Room, you can count on an arrestee before the end of the shift coming in high off drugs or drunk. And best believe they're disgruntled and mad because they were locked up. They're ready to fight the officers working in the Search Room, like we were the ones who locked them up in the streets of Baltimore. The good, but also the bad thing, about the Search Room is that it has cameras. That's good because if an arrestee becomes assaultive and start fighting with the officers, the camera records your actions and you may protect and defend yourself as long as you stay under the Use of Force Policy provided by Division of Corrections.

The bad thing about the camera is sometimes the arrestees really piss you off by doing or saying the dumbest things, and you just want to slap the shit out of them. If you're professional and with a courteous tone, say, "Sir Can you pass me your jacket, so I can search it?" And they throw it at you. Trust me, you'll get irritated really quick. I don't want to sound like the officers working in the search room are harsh or mean, but you must endure this foolishness for eight hours. Those cameras saved a lot of arrestees from getting back-hand slapped in the mouth. One of the rules, once you get locked up and come to BCBIC, is that you can't have contraband.

Now, for someone who just broke the law and got arrested, following rules may be a little difficult to understand, I guess. But rules are rules, so with those who don't want to give up their boots, we tell them, you can voluntarily give up your boots and they will go with your property, or we can forcefully take them and throw them away. Mostly, it's 2 out of 8 split. There's always that one or two, no matter what you tell them, they're just not going to follow rules of the institution. My thing is, either way you're going to lose, because rules are rules. Also, as stated earlier about the Search Room, if the arrestee has any money, we count all the bills and coins, give them a grand total and place the money in an envelope. We seal the envelope, we sign it, and they sign it.

There will be arrestees who come in with, let's say $40. But I guess, these are the pan handlers of the world because the $40 are all pennies, nickels, and dimes, and a few quarters. Counting $40, and all coins, is going to take a minute. That's enough of the Search Room, let's move on to the Intake Area.

There's usually like 3 to 4 male officers working back here, and a sergeant working the intake desk. There must be all male officers working in the intake area, because now the arrestees get a full strip-search before going up to one of the housing units in Security. A more thorough strip-search must be done in this area, because arrestees will try to hide contraband anywhere and everywhere. We would have the arrestees strip off all their clothes to be searched. Then we'd do a body search by having them raising their hands and arms, running their hands through their hair lifting up their private areas, and turning around squatting and coughing. The procedure of squatting and coughing, believe it or not, is where we find most of their contraband.

We are not surprised, but amazed when a cell phone and charger falls out of an arrestee's butt, ass, or rectum if you want the word to be politically correct. The rectum I guess, they think is a great place to hide their drugs, cigarettes, and lighters as well. I can't make this stuff up (lol), I see it firsthand, all the time. Now there are some days where you can go a whole day without any incidents, but then there are days you'll get one or two Assholes, (excuse my language) whose job is to come in and just ruin your whole day. That's just the stress of corrections.

For some of these arrestees, reality starts to set in. Being brought in to BCBIC in handcuffs or flex cuffs. Then booked, charged, photographed and fingerprinted. Waiting in a crowded cell with barely enough room to sit down. Having to give up all your personal belongings and then to be search for any drugs or weapons. Yup, Mr. Arrestee, you being locked up was mentally starting to take focus in your mind.

Let me say this before I forget, my hat goes off to all the Baltimore City Police Department and the duties they must perform. But some

(Not All) lie to these guys or arrestees by telling them "I am locking you up, but the charge is small, you'll do a walk through at the BCBIC, but you won't see a Court Commissioner and they will release you in a couple hours." Yeah right (lol). You're going to walk through all right, you're going to walk through the whole process like everyone else; and 9 times out of 10 you're going to see a Court Commissioner. I say 9 times out of 10, because they're on that few cases like disorderly conduct that the State's Attorney might deem a petty charge and release you within 24 hours, without seeing a Court Commissioner. Rare, but it could happen.

So now, we have this arrestee thinking he or she was getting this so-called walk-through. Sitting in a booth, seeing a Court Commissioner. The Court Commissioner declared the charge he committed is feasible to get a bail. Right after them seeing the Court Commissioner, they come in the back and Intake. Now we got to deal with this upset arrestee who thought he was just going to be here for a couple hours. Once again, some cooperate, and some we must deal with accordingly. I could never understand why they're mad at us. One, you did the crime, two, the police locked you up.

After the search is done we give the guys an opportunity to take a shower. Now remember, they make it back to intake after waiting in a crowded cell for the past 12 to 24 hours. And judging by the smell of these guys it's no telling when the last time they had taken a shower was. Beyond stinky. But, like I said, we give them the opportunity. Of course, there are some, after the strip search, who just put back on their clothes and say "I'm good with the shower, I'll take it later, once I'm in Security. Yeah right, you nasty Fucking Bastard. (Excuse the language). Hope you don't get a cell mate who likes to keep himself clean. He might beat you up as soon as you walk into the cell for smelling like that. Disgusting.

A Correctional Officer can never master a post. I say that, because you learn to deal with different problems, attitudes, and drama from inmates or arrestees on a daily basis. So, I say you won't master your post, but you'll be good at what you do. But on the same hand, doing the same duties on a constant and daily basis, makes you lax. And this is not the career to be lax in.

This job, I call it babysitting, because that's what it seems like sometimes. If you're watching a baby, who just learned to crawl or walk, you got to keep your eyes on them, because once they think you're not looking or paying attention to them, they're gone. Sad, but true, the same rules apply to working corrections. We *are* babysitting, just grown men and women. If you don't keep your eyes on these inmates, they're fighting, stealing from each other, bullying each other, and just like a baby who has learned how to escape out of their playpen, these arrestees and inmates will escape out of any jail, if you don't properly watch them.

Getting me through my adult-sitting career in Corrections is doing different things and learning different areas of this institution. Which brings me to the next post I begin to work in at BCBIC. The supervisors needed officers to go take a finger printing course at the Divisions of Corrections Headquarters, where I got certified fingerprinting-taking and techniques. After I, of course successfully passing the course.

I started to get assigned working in the Fingerprint and ID Room. Now, to have this certification and to do fingerprints in any other career probably will be a fun thing to do. But in corrections, especially a place like this, oh my goodness... it's challenging. Imagine trying to take a person's fingerprints, who is super-high on drugs. They're jittery, scratching, and nodding off in a sleep-like coma. Or, you have the ones that come in drunk. The alcohol is wreaking out their pores and their breath is smelling like fresh vomit. And then, trying to get a front and side view photo of a high on drugs or drunk arrestee makes you say to yourself "they don't pay me enough for this". Yes, it was challenging, to say the least.

The next two posts I started to learn, are the ones that definitely made me think of what is going on in Baltimore City, or what is going on in American Cities. The first is the Court Commissioner's Hallway (also known as A Line Corridor). Now, let's paint the picture. There are usually three officers working this post. All in a hallway with about six holding cells on the A Side, and about six holding cells on the B Side or Booking Side.

Our job is to seek and find arrestees out of these overcrowded holding cells. Once we find them, one by one, we place them in a Court

Commissioner Cell to find out their fate. After they're done with the Court Commissioner, we take them out of the booth and put them in the Intake Cell for the Intake Officers to come get them, or to the release area for the Lieut. or the Sgt. to do their part in releasing them. Now I say, this is one of the posts that has me thinking *what's going on*, in our American Cities or Baltimore City because I work here, is that *these holding cells Stay Packed.* Packed with residents of Baltimore City, I'm sure, with people who can be doing something better with their lives, instead of getting arrested.

Now, don't get me wrong, some of these guys have done some terrible crimes that they needed to be locked up and thrown under the prison for the rest of their lives. But then, there are some that say, "They were in the wrong place at the wrong time". There are the ones who say, "I was walking down the street on this hot summer day. I was drinking a bottle of beer that was in a brown paper bag. Instead of the police officer saying that's not allowed and for me to pour it out, the police officer ordered me to sit on the curb, and the next thing I know I'm in Central Booking."

The arrestee told me, I guess the rules change for Preakness at Pimlico Racetrack, or for the Orioles and Ravens' game, when everybody was walking around with open containers of alcohol. Then there are the ones I think just like to be locked up. Here's an example: Let's say the police locked you up for loitering or trespassing. You're walking or sitting somewhere that clearly has a no Loitering or

Trespassing sign. Okay, the police locked you up and you come to BCBIC and eventually you see a Court Commissioner for your crime.

The Court Commissioner tells you that's a petty crime and for you to stay out of that area. Well what the Hell, (excuse my language) a week later you get locked up for the same dam thing. Hold up, it doesn't stop there. The Court Commissioner says, "Wait a minute, weren't you just in here last week". But the Court Commissioner is still a little lenient and tells the arrestee, "I'm giving you a bail for your crime, but is only for $100." So, the arrestee gets a phone call, calls a family member or friend to pay the $100 bail and he is on his way.

But it doesn't stop there. About a month later, you see the same guy again. "What the Hell!" is what I say to him, "What you get locked up for this time?" The arrestee says, "The police says he saw me smoking weed." My response was, "Well, were you?" His reply was, "It was just a little piece of a joint, laying on the ground beside me and he says it was mine." The arrestee asked me, "So, Officer Bryant, do you think the Court Commissioner is going to give me a bail for that?" My response was, "I'm not sure what kind of bail you're going to get for a little marijuana joint lying on the ground beside you, but being that you were here three times in the last month is not helping your case either."

We both had to laugh at that. Laughing he said, "You're right about that C O. If I hadn't been working here, I could not imagine the amount of people who get locked up daily." Men and women. Women come to Central Booking, as well, and they get the same process as men (booked, finger printed, ID, and they also see a Court Commissioner). The only difference is, if they get a bail for the arrest or charge, they are not housed at Central Booking. They are escorted over to a female facility next-door at Baltimore City Detention Center.

There's only a few male correctional officers who work on the female side of Baltimore City Detention Center, but from what I hear from the Officers who work over there, is that the female arrestees or inmates are worse than the men. The next part of BCBIC I have learned to work, I think is the one post that irritated me the most. And that is the Male Sally Port. Oh, my goodness, it's like never-ending. The police wagons and cars pull up, and here come the arrestees. It is sad to say, but crime pays. The crimes and the foolish things people do on the street keeps me and my other correctional staff employed. But damn, they keep coming and coming and coming.

Like I said before, if I hadn't worked here I would never have known so many people get locked and brought here, on a daily basis. Just as soon as you sit down for a quick break, here comes another van with about 5 to 6 guys getting off. It takes no time for the benches to get full. The term, *if you can't do the time don't do the crime*, starts right here. My phrase is *if you can't do the time in, don't come in here crying*.

It's while sitting on these benches; the crying and the complaining begins. C.O., these cuffs are too tight. My response, "Okay, I can't take them off. After you see the nurse, the officer will cut them off in the search room." Boo Hoo Boo Hoo. C.O., I got to go to the bathroom. My response, "Okay, as soon as you see the nurse, someone from the search room will cut off your cuffs and take you to the bathroom." Boo Hoo Boo Hoo. C, O., I'm hungry as shit, ya'll got any bag lunches around? My response, "They may have some in the search room, but I'm not sure. Not to be smart, but why you didn't eat before you got locked up?" (lol). Boo Hoo Boo Hoo C.O., are ya'll crowded. Now what I want to say is; "By the fucking line outside and both benches are full, what the fuck you think?" But excuse my language and I try to keep it professional, I just simply say "Yup, just a little crowded (lol). Boo Hoo Boo Hoo.

The questions keep coming in and go on and on and on. *Irritating to say the least*. There are three shifts here at BCBIC. 7 to 3, 3 to 11, 11 to 7. In a 24-hour period there may be an average of 75 to 100 guys that come though this Sally Port of Baltimore City Booking and Intake Center, on a daily basis (and that's just the men's side. I'm not even counting the woman's side). Some days may be more than that. We're open 24 hours a day, seven days a week, so do the math, that's a huge number of people getting locked up on a daily, weekly, monthly, yearly basis. Crime pays.

CHAPTER SEVEN

FINALLY, C.O.3

I thank God, that the woman I married is gorgeous, intelligent, and hard-working in the medical field as an Office Manager. Working at a major hospital, she is going through some employment challenges of our own, dealing with doctors and the staff she manages. We're able to raise our children as a two-parent household with salaries. By me being the man of the house, I try to supplement my income by working overtime on my job. It is, no doubt, sometimes I hate being here; but working overtime really puts a boost in my moderate paycheck. Especially in this economy, where things are going up all the time.

Most of the overtime I work here at BCBIC is done in the Security part of the institution. It normally consists of hospital details, or escorts and reliefs. If an inmate is extremely sick or got hurt while in the institution, and has to be admitted at a hospital, two officers have to sit in the hospital room with him or her, until they are released from the hospital. Easy overtime money. Escorts and reliefs is another easy gig in Security for overtime, because all we do is escort inmates throughout the institution and relieve officers on their posts for their lunch breaks.

When I work in the Security side of Central Booking, it reminds me a lot of my old institution. Glad I chose to work in the Booking Area, when I first got here, instead of Security. And speaking of my old Institution, I see I wasn't the only one burnt out because there are other officers from MRDCC, who transferred here as well. We sometimes reminisce about MRDCC. We always agree that the employees were cool to work with, and still to this day, some are still close friends; but the way the institution was run really stressed me the hell out.

Its 2010 and President Barack Obama gets the Affordable Care Act (some may call it Obama care) past. It helps thousands and thousands of Americans get health insurance that they really can't afford, or their jobs supply don't it. Now, notice I said 'Americans'. Some people truly believe that Obama Care is just for poor blacks. Nope. The Affordable Care Act, I feel, was a great idea because it gave healthcare to any American who needed it, - that means all races - a chance to get health care for themselves, their children, and even the elderly, who did not have any healthcare, but truly needed it.

Another reason I remember 2010 is, because Apple released the iPad and it seemed like everyone had to have one, except me (lol). In 2010 I remember I was really focused on this Sergeant's exam. I wanted to get the best score and interview I could possibly get. I have over 14 years in my career in the MD. Department of Corrections. Working as a correctional officer, there are some officers who get promoted that have less than 10 years in.

Then there are some officers that really have no desire to get promoted to sergeant, and they do their whole 20 years of employment and never feel the need to get promoted. Being a sergeant is something I want to accomplish before I retire. So, I set my goals to have the best score I can possibly get. The sergeant exam is given once a year, and hundreds of correctional officers from all institutions gather to take the test. Once it's taken you receive your results in about three to four weeks.

When I received my test results in the mail, I can't lie I got a little nervous. I opened the letter and, Yes, I received a good score. That's one weight lifted off my shoulders; now all I have to do is study for the upcoming interview. So, I studied as much as I can so when this interview comes I'll be ready. But in between time, another opportunity presented itself to me. I was asked by the Training Department training coordinator if I would be interested in becoming a firearms instructor for this institution. I guess they noticed my near-perfect scores when we do our annual range training. *Hey, I was a sharpshooter in the Army.*

So, I took them up on their offer to become an institutional Firearms Instructor. This made me feel like I was moving up in the world of Corrections. A few officers and I went out for a one-week training course to become a firearms instructor. It was pretty intense and fast-paced, but we all got through it and became official firearms instructors. Now when I go to the gun range, I'll be helping teach other correctional officers on using the firearms that we have in this department. After the instructor's firearms course was over, we had to go out to our Training Academy to take a one-week course on how to teach in a classroom setting. I think the course was called 'Teach to Teach', but don't quote me on that.

The next thing that happened to me was a Blessing in disguise, but at the time, I thought to myself, *this is not what I signed up for (lol).* The Training Coordinator told me that all firearms instructors not only have to teach out at the range for firearm classes, but also had to do In-service classes, as well. In-service classes are subjects that all correctional staff must be taught and tested on, annually.

Once a year, all staff, some may say: go through the torture of sitting in some fun, but mostly boring classes, to be taught and show proficiency on things that we do or may have to do on the job. The classes assisted of First Aid and CPR, Use of Force, Suicide Prevention, Ethics and Professionalism, Restraints, Prison Rape Elimination Act aka PREA, and so on and so on. Now, what threw me off, at first, is I'm not really a talker, let alone someone to stand in front of a class and teach. But, if I wanted to stay a firearm instructor, I had to help in teaching these classes.

All these years in corrections, I sat as a student in these classes. The thought of being an Instructor never crossed my mind. But hey, what the heck, so I did it. I had to go to a course called 'How to be an Instructor out at the Maryland Correctional Academy' in a couple of weeks. Remember, I said Blessing in disguise, because it didn't stop there. Everything was happening so fast, because while at work one day, I received a call saying that I need to schedule my Sergeants interview. When they say prayer works, it really does. So nervous, but confident, I went to my Sergeants interview. Now this is where I say to be asked to teach In-service classes was a Blessing in disguise. For the most part, the questions they asked me on the interview were pretty much what I studied for and will be teaching these In-service classes.

Once again, nervous, but confident, I breezed through the questions that were asked of me, with no problem. The last question the panel asked me is, *why I would make a great Sgt.* I remember giving them brief accomplishments of my 14 years in corrections. All that, I have learned. So, making sergeant will be a great accomplishment for me, now that I am a Firearms and In-service instructor. I mentioned that most of the instructors are sergeants and I, myself, would like to teach as the rank of Sergeant. And then I gave them the usual, or how I have a good attendance record; and since I'm now an Instructor and former Military, I always try to maintain a professional appearance. (Hopefully I said the right things, and these are the answers the panel wanted to hear.

After all the interviews were done, a few days went by. And guess what! I must've said the right things and presented myself the right way, because I GOT IT. Finally, I made Correctional Sergeant a.k.a. CO3. Finally, it took me a while, but I got it. I must admit that there was a little jealousy and tension amongst my peers. This, is understood I guess, because thinking about it, even though I got over 14 years in corrections, I had only been here at Central Booking for a little over four years. I was told by other sergeants that I will have some officers who will resent me getting promoted. We call these people-haters. These are the same officers who never took a sergeant's exam; who were always absent or come to work late, and always complain about everything that goes on at the job. Don't hate, appreciate… but who cares.

When I first got promoted, I had to go to the 3 to 11 shift. Three steps forward and get one step back. And honestly, I hated this shift. It wasn't necessarily the officers who I hated on this shift, because everyone was pretty much cool, and the 3 to 11 shift stuck together like family. It was just the time of day. Working midday seemed like you missed everything that goes on in the evening. I feel the 3 to 11 shift is for single young officers who like to get off work at 11, still have time to go out and party; and can sleep off the hangover, because they don't have to be to work until 3 o'clock the next day.

Unless I am on my off day, my family, once again, hardly sees me because the kids are at school and my wife is at work during the day, and usually is asleep by the time I get home. This sucks, but getting promoted, some sacrifices come with it. I must say, this was a great year for the fact that I did get promoted… but it gets better. After a few months on the 3 to 11 shift, the Training Coordinator who is a Lieut. was possibly leaving her position for a possible promotion. The Assistant Training Coordinator who is a Sgt. was getting promoted to

Lieutenant and will be taking her position as the training coordinator. (I'm hoping you are following me on this. So, I was asked if I would l be interested in being the assistant training coordinator for Central Booking. Yes, Yes, Yes, I think was my answer. That means I'll be working directly in the training office (I'll have my own desk), I would go back to the 7 to 3 shift, and get this, I'll be working Monday through Fridays with weekends and holidays off.

I am truly blessed. Of course, once again, there were some who congratulated me, but also hater-nation came out and it showed their hate; but once again, who cares. All within a little over a year, I became a Firearms Instructor, to being promoted to Sgt., to taking on a new position as Assistant Training Coordinator. Life is good.

As you may notice in my story I didn't mention a lot of names. It's not to be selfish, but this story is about me. But I must mention my mentor and my supervisor, when I took the position as Assistant Training Coordinator. The Training Coordinator, at the time, was Lieut. V. Winborne. The office we share is probably the smallest room in the whole Central Booking, but we clicked mentally and spiritually; we made the small space work. She taught me how to become a better instructor, which was encouraging for me, a person who most people say that I'm quiet. She had no problem teaching and critiquing me on my job, as well as showing me what she does as Training Coordinator, in case she wasn't there.

Not too many people, especially your supervisor, will show you what they do. I guess it's the fear that you may take their job. But she wanted me to know everything that was going on in that office. Being an Assistant Training coordinator, not only did I have to teach in the in-service classes at least twice a week, but I also helped schedule all Correctional staff who had to go to these in-service classes. Being we were both range instructors, from time to time, will still go out to the gun range and assist on qualifying officers with the weapons we used in Corrections. Being that our office area was small, every little thing or assignment that we had to do outside the office, I was ready to go. There were little office duties that had to get done, like grading and filing tests and laminating IDs or certification cards.

There was a lot of tedious work, which kept me busy all day; but just being in that little office, sometimes I felt a little claustrophobic. Once a month, all the Baltimore Region Training Coordinators and Training Coordinators Assistants have a meeting with the Baltimore Regional Training Coordinator. These meetings were very important. For liability reasons, and also, the State of Maryland Corrections needed everyone to be up to date and proficient in their annual training. So, each month, each institution's Training Coordinators gave their status report on who was trained and who needed to be trained, a.k.a. accountability. We also discussed ways on how to make the training more enjoyable.

Of course, with any job, veterans who'd been there 10 or 15, even 20 years, hated training. So, in these meetings, we discuss and implement new ideas we can present, and try to establish a new environment to where, even the old-timers would appreciate. We must always teach all core classes, like First-Aid, The Use of Force, applying Restraints, Suicide Prevention, etc. And, I admit some of these classes can be quite boring. Especially, if you're a veteran in corrections, sometimes you hear the same stuff over and over and over again. But, every year, we create lesson plans on new classes (Of course approved by the Division of Corrections) that can be taught to break up the monotony of the core classes.

We also implemented PowerPoint and games into our lesson plans to try to make things more fun. Most students (Officers) prefer to be taught hands on. I remember one year, we had a class on How to Manage Stress. At the end of the lesson plan or class, we gave it a full twist. We created a little game that we called "We're here to help you." So, these are the rules of how the game is played. We give everyone a piece of paper. That's 25 to 30 people in the class. We tell everyone if they have any problems in their life, work, with coworkers, or families to write it down on the paper and fold it up. Don't write any names on it, don't write any initials, and don't write what institution you work in because In-service classes had officers from all seven Correctional Facilities in the Baltimore region. Write your problem down and fold it up. The instructors in the class collected all the pieces of folded up paper, put them in a box or hat and mixed them all up.

Now, being that no one knows what or who wrote it, made this very interesting. We told the class, we are now Counselors, Psychiatrists, Friends - our brothers' and sisters' keepers. One by one, the pieces of paper were picked out of the hat and the instructors read them out loud to the class. As a whole, the class gave advice and counseling, on ways to help this person on the paper out with their problems. Sometimes, Prayer is given, as well. And believe me, there was some true counseling and advice given in the class. If you had financial problems, people gave some sound advice on how to save or manage their money.

If some women had babysitting issues, while at work, people in the class would network to some babysitters that were cost-effective and local in their area where they lived. If people had problems at work and didn't know how to get, or even ask for help, we gave resources on who to talk to or contact. We had single moms or dads who needed advice on raising their out of control teenagers, and some good mentoring advice was given. What made the game interesting is we were giving good advice and counseling to someone in the class, but you didn't know who. (Every now and then, it gets a little emotional, and you'd hear a "thank you" from somebody. You'd look for where that 'thank you' came from and you'd see a small tear come the person's face. Priceless).

Now sometimes, we'd get a gag question or problem. Every class always has a class clown (lol). Some out of the ordinary question that we thought was hilarious, but we'd still entertain it like it was a real question, because you never know. For instance, we'll pick a question out of the hat that reads, "I'm allergic to inmates, please help. What should I do?" The whole class would burst out laughing, but we entertained it, like it was a real question. Like I said, you never know. A response to that question may be, when you get off work, get you a red or white bottle of wine that will help you with that allergy (lol). Or, we'd get a question like, "My boyfriend hates me, because I didn't tell him I was married, how I can get him to get on board?"

Through all the laughter, people were actually looking around the room for the females, who were married, to try to figure out who would drop that question. This game got real serious, at times, to some officers and staff, because dealing with inmates on a daily basis can get very stressful. And that stress can grow and start to make you sick. So, this game allowed you to get things or problems off your chest anonymously and get some sound advice from your peers.

My time of working here in Maryland Corrections is getting short, and when I say short I mean short. Retirement is 20 years, so I got 17 in, 3 to go. Now, if I choose to, I can use Military time. Meaning the 3 years I served in the Army, I can tack that time on to this 17 years and leave today. Retiring from a job at the age of 47 sounds great. But, I decided to ride these last years out and get a full retirement from the State of Maryland.

It seems that after 2010 the Division of MD. State Corrections started hiring more officers. I guess, to cut down on overtime. There was a handful of officers making over $100,000 or close to it, but they were clocking in a lot of overtime a.k.a OT. That's more than most supervisors and administrators of Corrections make, and they weren't having that. A little jealousy and hate if you ask me. I guess they figured I went to college for four years - none were making $60,000 a year - and some of these officers were coming out of high school making between $80,000-$100,000. Oh no! Something has to be done. I know, let's hire more officers, so they can't boost their salaries in overtime.

So, more officers were hired, and it worked. They couldn't stop all the overtime, but just enough to where officers weren't making as much money. Frankly, I loved it. I felt like I was passing the torch to the new recruits coming in. I think back to 1993 when I first got hired and started at MRDCC. How the Training Sergeant showed me around the institution on my first day. How he taught the people I started with and in the pre-Academy classes. How he gave us a brief description and scenarios of what it's like to be employed in corrections.

I think back to those days, because now that's what I do as the Assistant Training coordinator; I help officers young in their careers get acclimated to their start in corrections. It brings me joy to see the new faces coming in. Lieut. Winbourne and I are like the cornerstones in helping them get started with their careers. All the training departments in the Baltimore region, come together and teach the new recruits their pre-Academy classes. I love teaching these classes because the new recruits are so intrigued by the stories we tell them and about our years we served in corrections. We give them the classes, take them on tours of their perspective institutions they'll be working at, and give them lots of words of encouragement; but being truthful and honest, at the same time by telling them that this job is not for everyone.

Yes, you applied for this job, passed the tests and got interviewed; and in a couple of days, you'll be going to the Academy, and we wish that you will do well. But when you start working the housing units by yourself, is where the real challenge comes into play. Officers have lost their jobs dealing with these inmates. They don't know you, or care about you. And there's nothing more embarrassing to be walked out of your job because you where compromised by an inmate. Inmates are master manipulators. They have nothing better to do but to watch you and try to figure out what type of officer you are. Are you the type of officer they can get to bring them in some cigarettes, drugs, or even a cellphone? Are you the over-friendly type, who can sit down being distracted with a 20-minute conversation, while there are other inmates in your area fighting or passing contraband?

If the inmate asks you for something, tell the truth, or just say no. Because once you say yes to anything, they will expect you to come through, and hound you every 10 minutes until it's done. We can sit here and think they won't pluck your last nerve, but they will. We always tell new officers to be yourself. If you weren't Superman or Superwoman on the streets, don't come in here thinking you can beat up 32 inmates out at recreation by yourself (lol). Any signs of trouble always calls for assistance. If you weren't a prom queen or king in high school, don't think you are one now, because these guys every day, all day, will tell you how good you look and how good you smell.

I don't think no males or female officers initially come to work looking for a date, by an inmate. That is harassment; so, end that quickly. But it never fails, we have had females with low self-esteem start being over-friendly, start writing inmates, giving the inmates their phone numbers, sending inmates naked pictures of themselves, and even going as low as to having sex with the inmate behind closed doors. All those are grounds of immediate termination, or even the State pursuing criminal charges against you. I have seen people come to work as officers, but by the end of the day, they're sitting in a cell, waiting to be processed for criminal charges. If you're hired for this career, try to be professional at all times, notice I said try to be. Example; an inmate will ask you to do something and you say No. Next thing he gets upset and calls you a stupid Bitch, Lazy Mutherfucking C O. or Whore Ass Officer, and you go from 0 to 100 really quick.

Remember, they have nothing else better to do, but to mess your whole eight-hour day up. But think about it, at the end of your workday, you're the one going home to your family and friends, eating what you want to eat, taking multiple showers, going to hang out, party, movies, restaurants, and sleeping in a warm comfortable bed… and not just reading a book in a little closet of a cell. So, don't let these guys take you there. A question is asked, if they start fighting, do I try to break it up? "Hell to the Naw." (lol) You sit back, grab some popcorn and enjoy the show. Just kidding that's not what you do. No, the truth is, you get on that radio quick, and call for assistance. Get some help to you first, because once you make that call, you are going to have C.O.'s coming from everywhere.

Those inmates fighting could be a set up to grab you or start fighting you. Remember, if you weren't one of the Marvel Avengers before starting this job, don't be a Super Hero now. Addressing the new recruits, I said listen, in 30 to 35 days you will be graduating from the Academy. The Division of Corrections, and your perspective Institutions want to see that everyone successfully passed the Academy. In order to do that, everyone must stick together, communicate, and study. If you're not a good test-taker, get to know people in your class and have study sessions. Before you all start becoming friends on Facebook (lol), start exchanging phone numbers to discuss what you may have missed in class. And even after the Academy in Corrections, we have to build a bond of a work family. Truth be told, some people may not have family and friends at home that they can count on when things get tough.

So, build that work friendship here; so, you always have someone to talk to in case of emergencies, or maybe have stressful situations. We're not asking you to like and love everyone you work with, but at least, be cordial with the people you work with. If you have a fight break out on your housing unit, of course you want everyone that can respond to get there with the quickness. But it's sad that there are some petty officers that would say, "I'm not running to that unit for a fight, Officer Jones is working there, and I don't like him." Ridiculous right, but I have heard of this happening. Also, leave work. Find things to do.

Some people let this job consume them, and next thing you know you're at home taking this job out on family members or kids. True stuff. Find a hobby or fun activities outside of this job. Now, don't let your hobby be drinking alcohol because you become an alcoholic really quick. (The class laughs) A student would of course ask, "Sgt. Bryant what's your hobbies?" Now that's none of your dam business (lol).

No, being honest, I myself really don't call it a hobby, I call it what brings me joy, outside of these institutions. First and foremost, I pray a lot. Now, I don't claim to be super religious, but praying helps keep me sane.

Next, it's my family, mom, wife, all my kids, sisters, nieces and nephews, aunts and uncles, and all my external family members. It makes me happy when we're all together, and for me to know everyone is safe and enjoying life. Winter and Fall, hey it's football season, Go Ravens! Spring and Summer, I get on my Harley Davidson Motorcycle and get some wind therapy with friends.

And last, but not least, even though my wife doesn't like the smoke, but a fresh Cigar and some Crown Royal Apple, can make you say, *satisfying*. Oh yeah, when I can get there, I go to the gym to work out, from time to time. These inmates, during recreation and outside yard, work out and exercise, so I try, and you should also try to stay fit. Notice I said *try* to stay fit.

That's pretty much it, remember there is life after the eight hours of this job, and so don't let your eight-hour shift consume you. Well said, Sgt. Bryant, well said. All the other Training Coordinators, Assistance and Instructors shared their views, experiences, and hobbies with the new hires, A.K.A rookies. And of course, with all new hires, they sat there intrigued and inspired to work. And listen, then I said to the class, "The beautiful thing about talking to you new hires, or should I say, new officers, is that we get to know you a little bit about you, before you go to the Academy. And after you graduate in 4 to 5 weeks all the training departments from all the regions come out to the Academy and congratulate you for completing the course. I like to eat so we have a big luncheon that day as well. Yum Yum.

After the graduation, excuse my language but the shit gets real. Some veteran officers would tell you new officers, once you get back to your respective institutions, "All you learned in the Academy, forget about it. That kind of statement is right and wrong to say to you. Yeah, the Academy gives you all the basics of Corrections, learning policies and procedures, etc.; but to actually work in these housing units by yourself, you'll learn really quick... it's a different beast. You'll feel that what you learned in the Academy has gone out the window. Not true, always stick with the basics, learn and ask questions and build on that.

Never be a person who thinks they know it all, because there are still veterans here learning their job every day. Also, I'll give you a real show 'nuff (that's slang for sure enough) status. If I have six people from my institution graduate from the Academy, within three years, I say again within three years, one will get compromised by an inmate, and start sneaking in contraband. They will get fired or suspended, so that's one down.

One will get fired or suspended for not coming to work on time, always calling off, or they just don't care about that job. So out of the six, now we have four. One will definitely prosper, intrigued to move up the ranks quickly. They'll jump from Sgt. to Lieut. to Capt., and the haters will be like, "Damn what did they do, or who did they do to move up the ranks that fast?" This is true stuff. One will use their job as a steppingstone, to seek other employment in the State of Maryland, or elsewhere whether it's a State Police, State Psychologists, or Counselor, etc. And then there's two, now these two are pretty much your normal Officer in Corrections. They come to work to make money and to support themselves and family. They love overtime. For the most part, they follow policies and procedures of the institution, and learn the job with proficiency, so at the end of the day they go home safe. I can't speak on every Officer in Corrections, I can only tell you the truth on what I've seen and experienced over the years.

120

On the outside looking in, people have no idea what is like or the crap Correctional Officers put up with, on a daily basis. There are good days when you tell yourself I got paid for this, and then there's bad days that make you want to get off and either start looking for a new profession or want to slap the first person you see. My prayers go out to all the families of the officers, who were killed in the line of duty working corrections, or hurt by inmates, who just have no respect for authority let alone for his or her own life. Taking this career is a challenge, for you never know how your day is going to end. All you can do is make it your duty to go home the way you came in, and also to watch each other's' back, attempt to be professional at all times; and you may not like him, but to try to get along with your co-workers who you'll see have 1001 different personalities (lol). "Good Luck Rookies."

While months away from doing my 20 years in corrections. (15 as an Officer, 5 as a Sergeant) I started to express to my fellow officers and supervisors: "When I get within four months to go, I'm going to start looking for another job. Even though I'll be eligible to collect a retirement pension from the State of Maryland, it's really not much to live on - especially trying to support a family - and I'm only 47 years old. Thank God, after 20 years in this job, I'm still healthy and also look good (lol). If I didn't mention this earlier, my wife and I bought a house right across the Maryland line, in the state of Pennsylvania. Hey, what can I say, homes are half the price in Pa. than in Md. and the commute to work is a straight shot down 83 N. which takes me only 40 to 45 minutes to get to work.

Not bad. So, I started applying for new careers, since it was getting close to my 20 years in the Maryland State of Corrections. The one job that seemed promising was the York County Sheriff Department. Oh yes, I got the interview and the psychological tests and a physical agility test, for which I am 47 years old; and that pretty much took a toll on this 47-year-old body, physically. But hey, I was a soldier from the United States Army, so I got through it. The process was slow, so as a backup, and since I got a lot of Correctional experience, I was at one of the State of Pennsylvania Human Resources Offices looking over job announcements, so I applied for the Pennsylvania Division of Corrections, along with some other jobs. And with all the jobs I applied for, through applications or resumes, guess which one called first.

CHAPTER EIGHT

GLUTTON FOR PUNISHMENT

I remember it like it was yesterday, I stood in roll call, and it was mid December 2013 at 6:48 am. My heart was pounding a mile a minute. After the Captain and Lieutenant gave their information from the previous shift and information for this shift, the captain asked, "Are there any questions or concerns?" I without hesitation raised my hand. All eyes are now focused on me. I would like to thank my fellow officers, not all just some of you. (lol), for all the support and friendship over the years.

There will always be a difference in ages, culture, and different personalities; but please continue to try to support one another and watch each other's back. I say all that, to announce today is my last day in Corrections at Central Booking; and I will be retiring from the State of Maryland today. So, thank you all, God bless you, and have a great day. A round of applause filled the hallway. Also, there were a lot of looks of disbelief and surprise. For the rest of day, they I got a lot of staff wishing me congratulations.

People asked all day why I didn't let them know earlier so they could give me a farewell party, cake, and balloons. My answer was, "That's not what I wanted. It's traditional when you get 20 years on a job, some people want balloons, cake etc. I just wanted to get up, come to work and say I'm done. My good friend, and also supervisor, still managed to put together a luncheon with coworkers from the training department and they gave me a beautiful Gold Invicta watch that I still wear till this day, when I get dressed up and on special occasions. My friends asked do I have any regrets for leaving. My response is no.

Even though I am retiring from the state of Maryland and will receive a pension check every moth, I'm only 47, still feel good about myself mentally and I'm still physically able to work. I still have a family to support. My wife has a stable income with her career, but at this day and age with her salary and my little pension, a household needs a two-salary income; so, I still must work. So, hopefully, one of these jobs come through, because the buyback cash the State of Maryland gave me for all my accumulated leave and sick time, is running out quick. (lol).

As I mentioned earlier, between the York County Sheriff Department and the State Department of Corrections in Pennsylvania, which one will call first. Well, this is a Glutton for Punishment, I thought. Welcome to Pennsylvania State Correctional Institution of Camp Hill or (SCIC). Hey, I undoubtedly did 20 years of Corrections and Maryland, downtown Baltimore City, at that. How bad can it be, right? We'll speed this up to the present, and after two years here, everything about Maryland Corrections, the two institutions that I worked at, too where I work at now, flip it. You may say, "What do you mean, flip it?" Well, as Slick Rick (an old-school rapper) said in the song "Children Story," Heeere We Go!

Let's start with the staff. In Maryland, the Baltimore and Jessup region of Corrections, the staff were majority black, or African-American, if you're politically correct. At Camp Hill (SCIC) the majority of staff is Caucasian. On my third day here, my new, of seven starting- out new careers at the State Correctional Institution of Camp Hill, we were given a tour of the facility. Not one building that I'm used to being in. But this facility that sits on acres and acres of land. The new group coming in with me consisted of two Blacks, two Latinos, two Caucasians, and one mixed race of Black and White (all military veterans).

Now, thinking about it, we were a very diverse group. We were escorted around this very large compound, which holds around 3400 inmates. As we walked past this building, called the Educational Building, a couple of officers were standing out in front of the building, and one of the officers yelled out "What's up new officers? It's about time they hired more black people!" *What in the world?* I thought to myself. The next thing that was different is that 65% of the staff from where I came from were female officers, compared to here where there are defiantly more male officers. Wow, that's a switch.

After 20 years in Maryland, corrections, that is just astonishing - the different things I see here in Corrections in Pennsylvania. My group and I, who I came in with, received our orientation classes, before going to the Academy. Yes, I got to go to the Academy. Unfortunately, Pennsylvania Corrections doesn't honor other states' Correctional time. It's kind of like I'm starting all over again. What I quickly realize is that the orientation and the Academy is nothing that I never heard before. Another thing I realize is the pay. Not only does PA Corrections get their annual raises one time, they also get a contract raise, pretty much every year; plus, on top of that, they get a clothing allowance in July, yes, every July (to buy new uniforms or boots).

So, doing a little calculating, I figure between six to eight years, I'll be making about the same amount of money here that I did in Maryland, during 20 years. Unbelievable. I should've given Maryland those three years of time I did in the military and gotten here three years ago. I can't believe Maryland's Correctional Union sucked. There were years and years we didn't get pay raises, at all. If you were a Maryland State Employee, the only ones who got raises of course was the Maryland State Police, mainly because they had their own union. And if something wasn't right with their pay or salaries, they stuck together, marched, and protest. That's how they got stuff done, they let their voices be heard.

Maryland Corrections unfortunately didn't have a lot of unity, and the administration would fire anyone who ever protested about their salary. Which meant years and years of no raises, pay cuts, and little advancements. Anyway, back here to SCIC, I have to really humble myself into coming into Corrections here. I never, to this day, acted like I know it all. It's like driving a brand-new car; even though you know how to drive, you still have to learn all the new features of the car. So, when my group of new officers and I went to the Academy, the verbiage was different, but it was still the same stuff that I have been teaching for the past three years and learning 17 years prior to that.

There are two things Maryland Corrections is ahead of in the Pennsylvania Corrections. One of those things is the Prison Rape Elimination Act a.k.a. PREA. It's an act or policy that helps protect inmates that are violated in some sought of sexual manner in the prison system. Maryland implemented this years ago. The second thing is the firearms we use. Yes, Maryland corrections used to use the 38 revolver, but transitioned to the Smith & Wesson 40 caliber. PA is still using the old 38 revolver… some say it's the pistol to rob stage coaches. And when we go on hospital details I'm not to mention what we do here different because I still work here and that may be confidential (lol). Other than that, everything is flipped around from what I am used to.

My group and I all passed Academy, and my journey with SCIC in Pa. begins. Now we started with seven in my group, but we lost one when we came back from the Academy. Now remember, I said things are different here. Officers are allowed to grow beards. I'm talking full grown beards. For you old-timers reading this, I'm talking ZZ Top beards (that's an old rock band with long beards for the new generation reading this). You couldn't do that in Maryland, unless you had a shaving profile.

Anyway, the group member that did not make it he was asked to shave or trim his mustache down by. He refused and was eventually dismissed. I couldn't understand, because he could have just trimmed it. It's hair, it would have grown back, and he'd still have his job. I'm guessing maybe it was his way of getting out and leaving corrections without looking like he had the fear of working here. When you first walk through these walls and gates of any institution it could be a little intimidating. But who am I to judge?

Once again, I'm in the training status. For the next year, we go through phases. Phase one, two, three, and four. Through learning and experience, we develop the skills on how this institution works. There are a lot of different posts here at SCIC, so we take on the challenges of learning their policies and procedures. Like I said, I still presently work here so I don't want to get into too many details about this institution, but I like to compare from where I came from to where I'm at. So first, I'll touch on the officers.

The majority of the officers here are Caucasian. Compared to the majority African Americans where I came from. There are a lot with long beards, compared to how we had to be clean cut and shaved. And some, I say, *some* uniforms look a little dusty. I said dusty. Now I don't mean to disrespect anybody, but the difference is that, in Maryland, we had to be sharp, pressed, badges in insignia shined and boots polished. Here at Camp Hill, it is like just make it to roll call one time, "you hear, cool, go to work". Going on a lot of these posts, even though I had 20 years as a Correction Officer in Maryland, I'm still new here, so I never was overly confident.

But as I go on different posts, officer always ask me, were you in the military, or what did you do before working here? I always found that question funny. Yes, I replied, I was in the military and now I'm a glutton for punishment, because I just retired from Corrections in Maryland. They often looked kind of surprised when I say that, but they can tell, even though I'm new here, this is not my first rodeo in doing this type of work. Now, I'm not going to bite my tongue for saying this, and let me make myself clear, not all, but some of these guys seem racist. Even though some try to hide it, but it is what it is. An example from many, even after being here a couple of months.

When officers know who you are, you can walk right by a few of them, say hello or how are you doing, and they give you no response, but just keep walking by. What the hell. My response should be, *I know you heard me fucking talking to you*. But I'm too mature and professional for that. Guess what! I'm not mad at you. Over the years I've learned, you are not born a racist, but I think you're just taught it. I remember all the way back in 83, when I was in the Army, there were Caucasians who lived in some parts of America, who they claimed never lived or had been around other races, but their own. And if you're taught to hate everyone that's not your kind or race you're brainwashed to hate. And this type of behavior goes on from generation to generation. Sad, but true.

The funny thing is that there are some African-Americans who are no better. I've seen African-Americans who are raised around nothing but African-Americans and feed off the hatred of if they hate me, I hate them. That's Craziness. The chain must be broken. I've had the pleasure and honor, to have worked at two places, where all people should unite and work together. These places are the Army and Corrections. If there were any type of wars, you would unite to become a military force to be reckoned with. The color of your skin, race, or religious beliefs, does not matter when bombs and bullets are flying over your head.

The slogan is 'an army of one'. Troops band together, when it's time to defend this country. Get this, the United States of America troops don't care if you're from the backwoods of Virginia or the Southside of Chicago, we are one. Same thing with corrections, when you hear over the radio, 'Officer needs assistance'! You run your ass off to get to that person's area. Black, white, brown, yellow; it doesn't matter. All you know is that an officer needs help.

This is 2016. I personally believe racism should have died in the 70's. The 60's was, well mostly, in segregation. The 70's era would begin the peace and love stage. Living in America, this is 2016, why are we still talking about racism? Why is this still being taught? There was an incident that happened in Baltimore City, where a black male died, while in police custody. All hell broke out in the city. Vandalism, riots, and protesters. To make a long story short, the news media focused on a group of protesters called *Black Lives Matter*. My opinion, and this is just my opinion.

At first sight of this group, I thought, *well, that's a little racist, don't all lives matter?* But in other states of America, more and more African-Americans were dying by the hands of law-enforcement officers. My moral to this story - *all lives do matter.* Even black lives. Once again, my opinion, the group wasn't established to be racist. The group are Americans, who want freedom and justice for all. Let's say you have a car and the car is named America. In order to drive America down the road effectively and efficiently, all four tires Black, White, Asian, and Latinos all must be inflated equally. If the black tire goes flat, does it matter? Hell yeah. Black tire needs the same air in it like the other tires. The Mechanic puts new tires on your car, they're not putting 32 psi in three tires and 10 psi in the fourth. No, they're going to be equal. It's part of the car, so it matters. The same way, with the Black Lives Matter movement, they're not trying to be different or separate, just equal.

Back to corrections. Let me take a moment to discuss the difference with the inmates here and from where I came from. Now this might amaze and surprise someone reading this book. The biggest difference in the population is that most of the inmates are Caucasian and White. I know the media have people thinking that jails are filled up with

Blacks and Hispanics. Well I'm here to tell you Caucasians get locked up to. But, no harm, no foul.

The thing that kills me is why America puts less money into education and more money into building new jails. Instead of investing in a child's future, they invest in supporting a grown man or woman in jail. Giving them three meals a day, proper medical attention, clothing, and a place to sleep at night. The inmate population here, is a little more respectful than what I had to deal with in Maryland. In Maryland, especially the old jail (BCDC), the housing units were loud. The inmates yelled out their cells, radios playing loud, cell doors and bars being covered with blankets or sheets, and officers getting cursed out, was routine. Here at SCIC was very different. Housing units are quiet. If you see an inmate standing at their door, officers yell out, "get off your gate or door, and they do it.

What the hell, I'm not used to that. In Maryland, if you tell an inmate to get off the door or bars, they would have done it, but you would've heard them say, "Fuck you C.O., I'll see you when I come out." Here at SCIC, when they go to eat, they walk on the premises to a huge inmate dinner hall. They sit down in an orderly manner, eat their food, and once finished, the officer directs them to leave. This happens three times a day, with little to no problems. Being this is a huge compound with some of these inmates doing their incarcerated time here. Daily, these inmates leave their housing units or blocks, and go on activities. Activities consist of the library, law library, church and the gym, in which they have weightlifting, basketball, softball, and soccer, outside when the weather permits.

As I mentioned, they have a full-size church on the premises, in which all religions practice their faith. No one is left out. And they even have a full-scale Muslim service on Fridays. Now these guys are incarcerated for something, so I don't picture them all as angels, because every now and then, there's a fight. Just like any other emergency, we respond, break it up, and they're taken to the restricted housing unit or RHU. So, some of these guys seem to lose their minds, and fight or stab each other. And occasionally, they want to fight or assault the correctional staff, for whatever reason. We rarely know what the fights are about. The bottom line is: our job is to protect each other and also protect the inmates from each other. Here at SCIC, the inmate population seems a little calmer.

My short time of being here at the State Correctional Institution at Camp Hill in Pennsylvania (SCIC), I haven't been tied down to one post. I've been on what's called the Walks. That's basically you're not working the same housing unit area every day and you're subject to be somewhere different every day. Reading this book, by now, you know that works for me. I got to move around. The advantage of working the same housing units or blocks every day is you get to be familiar inmates in your area. You know who's the troublemakers, who are the so-called gang members, who's the weak-minded inmates that get taken advantage of, who's the strong inmates trying to run anything, and mainly, who's the low-key inmates that are just trying to do their time and go home.

I go on the housing units, and inmates will ask me, what I think is a dumb question, and I know in my mind they already know the answer. But they figure that since I'm not a regular officer on the block, they may get a different answer from me. But what they don't realize, is I've been doing corrections for a long time, so I know the game. I'll entertain their moment to seek attention and answer the question, as best possible. I don't know what it is like to be in a jail cell about 20 hours a day, seven days a week, but I'm guessing that maybe they needed someone to talk to, and that person today would be me, since I am walking by.

Now, like I said earlier, there are some inmates here at SCIC, and they do their incarcerated time here. Most of them have little jobs here. Like working in the dietary department, working in the sanitation department, and the maintenance department. A few participate in the programs that are offered here, like a GED program to help you get your high school diploma; and they also have a barbershop program to help you get your barbers license. Now being that some of these guys have these extra privileges or perks, they seem to really forget the rules of being a prisoner in a state prison. They feel as if their cell doors are not supposed to lock if they come out. They feel they can come and go as they please. They think they are always supposed to get extra time on their visits, showers, phone time, eating, and activities.

No doubt about it, they do get a little leeway. But my thing is, if you're wanting all these extra privileges, stay out of jail. I'm not trying to sound cruel or mean, because people make mistakes in life and wind up here or in another prison across America. But if you find yourself locked up, follow the rules of the prison and not have the mindset that I'm special, because I'm doing my time at SCIC. Okay that's enough about talking about inmates, because 22 years of inmates irritate me really quick (lol).

This is 2016, and a lot is going on midway through the year. Something about me, I love all kinds of music. From gospel to old school rock 'n roll, from hip-hop to jazz, from reggae to R&B. That's why I was really hurt by the death of Prince. He was a master of his craft. He took his music to a whole another level. He put together generations of music that was loved by all. Now, if music can bring people together, why can't the presidential candidates?

Being that we are in 2016 we have had 7 ½ years of President Barack Obama. Let me make myself very clear, him being the first black President in America is not the reason I supported President Obama. I like President Obama because he brought the troops home from overseas missions, he provided healthcare (the Affordable Care Act) for people who desperately needed medical insurance, and he definitely lowered the employment rate. And some may not agree to the fact that he lowered the American deficit. And if you don't agree, I challenge you to check the numbers and statistics of the American economy from 7 ½ years ago until now, which at the time of writing, is 2016…before you foolishly say I don't agree.

I try to be realistic, and I remember when gas prices were almost $5 dollars and now are down to $2.50. I remember major companies and banks were getting bailout funds from the taxpayers. I remember people's homes were getting foreclosed at an alarming rate. So, for me once again, it wasn't because he was an African-American President, he pursued heavily on moving America forward. Sad, but his time in office is coming to a close.

So, I got the choices of Hillary Clinton or Donald Trump. Now people say Hillary will be a spinoff of Pres. Obama. So as a registered voter, I listen to her views. And I don't think she's a spinoff from Pres. Obama I feel she wants to move the country forward and I feel we as a country are getting better and moving forward compared to where we were at eight years ago.

While writing this book it is not time to vote and I'm not tied in on just one candidate. So, I also look at the views of Donald Trump, as well. Being an African-American male in America, depending on who you are, you might not believe that. But being a registered voter, I am not biased to one candidate; so yes, I really look at the views of Donald Trump, as well. Now, so far, not good. His views are building walls on the Mexican border to block out illegal immigrants, putting a ban on Muslim Countries for immigrants not to come into this country, and calling every candidate on both the Republican and Democratic side terrible names, is not a good start for me.

If you want my vote tell me how you want to move the country forward, not have a slogan, "Let's Make America Great Again." America has its faults, but I think we're great right now. Of course, everyone will not agree with me. I'm just one, out of billions of people living in America. We have to be positive and continue to move forward. My wife and I work hard to make a different decent salary to raise our kids. We are not rich by any means, but we are blessed to earn paychecks, have a nice house, transportation, food to eat, and clothes on our back.

I assure you, we are living the American dream. Which brings me to the question of, what is Trump trying to go back to? Slavery, World Wars, the Great Depression. The slogan should be, "Let's Make America Greater." Let's find ways to totally end racism. Let's find ways to prevent the high number of homelessness in America, instead of spending billions to house inmates in these American Prisons. Let's get to the root of the problem, and spend more money on all, I repeat on all American school systems, even the ones in inner-cities. Let's drastically lower costs on college tuitions or free college, so young adults can graduate and compete in corporate America. Fulfilling their dreams, instead of coming out of college, being thousands and thousands of dollars in debt. Let's create more jobs, and with more jobs the economy will grow.

The Constitution of the United States says, "We the People of United States." We need to get there. And to get there, as Americans, we should not judge people on how they look, or what's their skin color, or religion, or race, and what their sex is; but instead, we should love one another because they're American. We all come from different backgrounds or from other regions of the world. But dammit we are here now, let's live as one.

Funny thing is, some days when I go to work, my assignment of the day might consist of working an outside perimeter tower. And, while in the tower, I overlooked the inmates that come out for yard or outside recreation. I see yards and yards of basketball courts with inmates playing basketball. Teams are made up of all different races working together to win a game. Now granted, these guys are playing with boots on and it's an 85° summer day (the struggle is real). I don't see black guys playing against the white guys or Chinese playing the Hispanics, all the teams are mixed, men coming together as one to win. Why can't this country of Americans be that way? Yes, it will be a struggle, hell we have seen that already, but dammit if inmates can do it, so can we.

Still in the year 2016, I must take another moment for the loss of a great one, literally the greatest. Muhammed Ali. This man not only was a champion in the boxing world, but a champion in humanity, in our communities, as well as an ambassador for the world. They say if you have an hour-long conversation with Muhammed Ali, only 10 minutes would be about boxing; the other 50 minutes would be about how to be better people and make the communities we live in better. He was a role model, not only to his children, but to kids of all ages, all over the world. He took a stand on what he believed in, and never gave up. Rest in peace the greatest of all time, Muhammed Ali.

As for me, I'm 50 years old (still looking good for my age, I must say) with 22 years in corrections. How much more can I do? Here, in order to receive a pension, you need 20 years or age 55. So, since I've already have been here for two years, and three months, I'll have the age in a couple of years to receive a pension, but not enough time in to receive a full pension. Thank God, I have a monthly pension, which includes health insurance, coming from retiring in Maryland. But that's not a whole lot, and my wife and I still have a mortgage, car payments, minimum bills, and two daughters getting ready to go to college.

So, to leave with just a few years in, is not really an option. Besides I'm not chasing the money, because once you finally leave this earth, you can't take it with you; but in the meantime, you would like to live comfortably. And I would like to leave some type of funds for all my kids to share (Damion, Aaron, Brittany, Jazmine, Lauren - that phrase is for you). SCIC is all about seniority and longevity. The longer you stay the more you make. And if I didn't mention it before, I think in about six years here, I'll be making more than I did in Maryland doing 20 years. That is sad, but true. Damn it, I should've left State of Maryland Corrections three years ago (lol). One thing is for certain, being 50 years old with 22 years in corrections, things with this job and things inmates say irritate me. I know some people make mistakes and wind up in jail, but what you are going to do different in life, not to come back.

Recently I heard one guy saying that he can't wait to get out. He said I'm going to get some weed, get him a bitch, and just lay back and chill. I've been doing this too long, not to let that statement slide. So, I said to him, "Did pursuing a job and leaving the drugs alone, slip your mind?" I said, "Please tell me you don't have kids." He laughed and said, "That's Fucked up, C O, but yes, I do." I say, "Listen, I didn't mean to sound disrespectful, but break the chain. Show your kids there's more in life than doing things that could possibly get you sent back to jail or killed. I don't care what got you here or how long you been here, but one thing I know for sure is that you're going to have a chance to get out of here. You will get released. So, when that time comes, do the right thing, not only for you, but for your kids. Think about it and don't fuck it up." (I am a C O and a counselor once again in PA. Corrections). Of course, I got the normal reply from the inmate. "You're right, C O. Your right." Damnit, sometimes these grown men listen… maybe. (lol)

So, I figure it's 2016. In 2022 I'll be 58 years old and have eight years here. And with my military buyback that would give me 11 years of PA. State time. By then my wife's and my bills should be minimal, and my youngest daughter should have graduated from college that year. Not sure what kind of pension I will have with 11 years of State of PA Corrections. But that can be calculated, the closer I get to that time. I'm also investing more money into this retirement plan.

My second option, and this is really pushing it, is to work until I'm able to receive Social Security. Now don't think that's crazy, because people do it all the time. That means I'll have to work until 2028, in which I'll have a grand total of 34 years in Corrections - 20 in Maryland and 14 here in the state of Pennsylvania. My military buyback will give me 17 years total of PA. State time. But like I said, that's pushing it.

I sometimes ask myself, *if I could change anything in my life, what it would be?* And I have to be honest with myself and say nothing. God has truly blessed me. I wrote about my life and 22 Years in Front of these Bars and Corrections. I'm by no means perfect and without sin. I have done bad things in my life, and with any unfortunate circumstances, I could have been writing a story about my life *behind* bars. In a cell, trying to keep a cellmate off my booty. Eating small portions of food that looked and smelled disgusting. Having officers dictate on when I can take showers, when I go to sleep, when I use the phone to talk to my family.

What seems minimal in our eyes, for inmates the enlightenment of the day is coming out their cells for recreation. That little time of recreation would not be good for me, because the whole time all I'd been thinking about is "damn I got to go back to that box of a cell."

I feel that no one truly knows their destination in life, all you can do is try to shape it as much as possible. Work also to pursue being the best you can be, and hope and pray if you have kids, they have accomplished their goals and dreams of their lives. It corrections the greatest career in the world? By no means, no.

But I am happy to have this career. It was a steppingstone from my years in the military and it was beneficial to me, for I have seen and learned. It was a feasible income to support my family and me. It gave me a different perspective on how America and their lawmakers of the land spend billions of tax payers' dollars toward men and women in jail instead of taking the same money to build up schools and colleges.

Like I said before, there always will be criminals, so you will always need prisons, filled with evil-doers whose life misfortunes got them sent to an American Correctional Intuition. But I would love more funding going into making all kids prepared for their future. That we strive to live in a land where every race, color, religion lives -in a land where there is nothing but peace, love, and respect for one another.

A past recording artist, Sam Cooke, sang "change is going to come." And the change starts with you. We can't go backwards and make America Great Again. We Are Already Great! Let's make America Greater! One more past great musical artist, Michael Jackson, sang, "I'm starting with the man in the mirror, I'm asking him to make a change, and if you want to make the world a better place, take a look at yourself and make that change."

Thank you for your time and support for reading my story. May God bless you and your family.

ABOUT THE AUTHOR

L ewis Bryant was born and raised in Baltimore, MD. He is currently living in York, PA. and still works within Corrections at State Corrections Institution Camphill.

He is Married with 5 children, 1 grandchild, and more grandchildren on the way.

Lewis is a new author with hopes and dreams of making the *New York Times Best Sellers'* list.

CPSIA information can be obtained
at www.ICGtesting.com
Printed in the USA
LVHW04s0027300818
588621LV00001B/7/P